YA
344.73
ENG

D0742054

TEEN RIGHTS AND FREEDOMS

| Driving

Teen Rights and Freedoms

I Driving

Sylvia Engdahl
Book Editor

GREENHAVEN PRESS
A part of Gale, Cengage Learning

GALE
CENGAGE Learning·

Farmington Hills, Mich • San Francisco • New York • Waterville, Maine
Meriden, Conn • Mason, Ohio • Chicago

Elizabeth Des Chenes, *Director, Content Strategy*
Douglas Dentino, *Manager, New Product*

© 2015 Greenhaven Press, a part of Gale, Cengage Learning

WCN: 01-100-101

For more information, contact:
Greenhaven Press
27500 Drake Rd.
Farmington Hills, MI 48331-3535
Or you can visit our Internet site at gale.cengage.com.

For product information and technology assistance, contact us at:

Gale Customer Support, 1-800-877-4253.
For permission to use material from this text or product, submit all requests online at www.cengage.com/permissions.

Further permissions questions can be emailed to permissionrequest@cengage.com.

Articles in Greenhaven Press anthologies are often edited for length to meet page requirements. In addition, original titles of these works are changed to clearly present the main thesis and to explicitly indicate the author's opinion. Every effort is made to ensure the Greenhaven Press accurately reflects the original intent of the authors. Every effort has been made to trace the owners of copyrighted material.

Cover Image © Sean Locke Photography/Shutterstock.com.

LIBRARY OF CONGRESS CATALOGING-IN-PUBLICATION DATA

Driving / Sylvia Engdahl, book editor.
    pages cm. -- (Teen rights and freedoms)
    Summary: "This timely new series examines a broad range of perceived, practical, or actual legal rights and freedoms impacting the daily lives of teens. Each volume focuses on a different right or freedom. Material is drawn from primary and secondary sources. Many volumes cover rights guaranteed under the Bill of Rights and how these rights are interpreted and protected in regards to minors"-- Provided by publisher.
    Includes bibliographical references and index.
    ISBN 978-0-7377-6997-5 (hardback)
    1. Teenage automobile drivers--United States--Juvenile literature. 2. Teenagers-- Legal status, laws, etc.--United States--Juvenile literature. I. Engdahl, Sylvia, editor of compilation.
    HE5620.J8D75 2014
    363.12'508350973--dc23
                                                                2014016648

Printed in the United States of America
1 2 3 4 5 6 7 18 17 16 15 14

Contents

A study by highway safety experts showed that although graduated driver licensing laws have decreased fatalities caused by sixteen- and seventeen-year-old drivers, they have increased them for eighteen-year-old drivers. This may be because eighteen-year-olds now have less experience than when full driving privileges were granted at age sixteen.

Foreword

*"In the truest sense freedom cannot be
bestowed, it must be achieved."*
Franklin D. Roosevelt,
September 16, 1936

The notion of children and teens having rights is a relatively
recent development. Early in American history, the head of
the household—nearly always the father—exercised complete
control over the children in the family. Children were legally
considered to be the property of their parents. Over time, this
view changed, as society began to acknowledge that children
have rights independent of their parents, and that the law should
protect young people from exploitation. By the early twentieth
century, more and more social reformers focused on the welfare
of children, and over the ensuing decades advocates worked to
protect them from harm in the workplace, to secure public education for all, and to guarantee fair treatment for youths in the
criminal justice system. Throughout the twentieth century, rights
for children and teens—and restrictions on those rights—were
established by Congress and reinforced by the courts. Today's
courts are still defining and clarifying the rights and freedoms of
young people, sometimes expanding those rights and sometimes
limiting them. Some teen rights are outside the scope of public
law and remain in the realm of the family, while still others are
determined by school policies.

Each volume in the Teen Rights and Freedoms series focuses
on a different right or freedom and offers an anthology of key
essays and articles on that right or freedom and the responsibilities that come with it. Material within each volume is drawn
from a diverse selection of primary and secondary sources—
journals, magazines, newspapers, nonfiction books, organization

newsletters, position papers, speeches, and government documents, with a particular emphasis on Supreme Court and lower court decisions. Volumes also include first-person narratives from young people and others involved in teen rights issues, such as parents and educators. The material is selected and arranged to highlight all the major social and legal controversies relating to the right or freedom under discussion. Each selection is preceded by an introduction that provides context and background. In many cases, the essays point to the difference between adult and teen rights, and why this difference exists.

Many of the volumes cover rights guaranteed under the Bill of Rights and how these rights are interpreted and protected in regard to children and teens, including freedom of speech, freedom of the press, due process, and religious rights. The scope of the series also encompasses rights or freedoms, whether real or perceived, relating to the school environment, such as electronic devices, dress, Internet policies, and privacy. Some volumes focus on the home environment, including topics such as parental control and sexuality.

Numerous features are included in each volume of Teen Rights and Freedoms:

- An annotated **table of contents** provides a brief summary of each essay in the volume and highlights court decisions and personal narratives.
- An **introduction** specific to the volume topic gives context for the right or freedom and its impact on daily life.
- A brief **chronology** offers important dates associated with the right or freedom, including landmark court cases.
- **Primary sources**—including personal narratives and court decisions—are among the varied selections in the anthology.
- **Illustrations**—including photographs, charts, graphs, tables, statistics, and maps—are closely tied to the text and chosen to help readers understand key points or concepts.

- An annotated list of **organizations to contact** presents sources of additional information on the topic.

- A **for further reading** section offers a bibliography of books, periodical articles, and Internet sources for further research.

- A comprehensive subject **index** provides access to key people, places, events, and subjects cited in the text.

Each volume of Teen Rights and Freedoms delves deeply into the issues most relevant to the lives of teens: their own rights, freedoms, and responsibilities. With the help of this series, students and other readers can explore from many angles the evolution and current expression of rights both historic and contemporary.

Introduction

Since the middle of the twentieth century, a major rite of passage in the lives of American teenagers has been getting their driver's license. Many have looked forward to their sixteenth birthday as the date on which they qualify; some even taking their driving test on that day.

Recently, fewer teens than in the past have been getting their licenses as soon as they are of eligible age. Several reasons have been suggested for this trend. An important one is the state of the nation's economy; driving a car has become more and more costly due to soaring gas prices, as well as the expense of buying, maintaining, and insuring an automobile. Insurance rates for all of a family's cars increase significantly (sometimes even doubling) if there is a teen driver in the household—even if the teen never drives those cars—unless the teen personally owns a car with a separate insurance policy. Furthermore, driver education classes, which were formerly free, have been dropped from many high schools and must be paid for by the student. Families hard hit by the recession have little money to spare for nonessentials, and after-school jobs have become more difficult for teens to find. A study by the US Public Interest Research Group (USPIRG), however, found that cities with the biggest declines in driving did not have higher unemployment rates, so whether teen driving will increase as the economy improves remains to be seen.

Financial considerations are not the only reason many teens delay getting their driver's license. The social life of today's young people is less centered on cars than it used to be, and having one's license no longer provides the status it once did. Some observers believe that because teens are constantly in touch through cell phones and other electronic devices, they do not feel as much need for face-to-face contact as they did in the past. Studies by the University of Michigan's Transportation Research Institute found that a higher proportion of Internet users was associated with a lower rate of licensed young drivers in the countries studied. "Today, teens need look no further than Facebook or other social networking sites to connect with their friends," blogs Sarah Klein in *The Online Mom*. "They can also chat and play video games live. And they constantly text, sending as many as 10 messages an hour. There is simply less need, maybe less desire, to be able to grab the [car] keys and go," she notes.

Some teens say they are just too busy to learn to drive and to take the driver education courses now required. Others are concerned about the environmental impact of motor vehicles and prefer to use alternate forms of transportation. But since in many areas no public transportation is available, this applies to comparatively few who would formerly have driven a car. Still others have no need to drive because their parents are willing to take them wherever they have to go. Parents have become more concerned about the dangers of teen driving in recent years, and laws have been passed to keep young drivers from engaging in behavior known to be especially risky, such as talking or texting on a cell phone—activities most teens prefer to freely engage in and do not want restricted.

It has been suggested that teens are delaying getting their licenses because of these laws, known as graduated driver licensing (GDL) laws, which place restrictions on the use of cars by drivers under eighteen. Far more supervised driving practice is required than in the past, and even after a teen driver passes the driver's test, the license is only an intermediate one that in most states does not allow driving after dark or with any passengers other than family. Some experts believe that many teens feel it is not worth the time and money to learn to drive under these conditions, and are choosing to wait until they are old enough to be eligible for full licensing. Whether this is indeed the reason, experience has shown that those who do wait do not have the opportunity to hone their driving skills, and thus the laws' effectiveness has come into question.

GDL laws are intended to reduce the number of fatal accidents caused by young, inexperienced drivers, and they have been successful in this regard among sixteen- and seventeen-year-olds. Statistics have shown, however, that fatal accidents among eighteen- and nineteen-year-old drivers have increased since GDL laws have been in effect. This may be because some teens do bypass the extended learning stage and are therefore still as inexperienced as a younger teen when first licensed. On the other hand, it may be that there just is no net benefit to the laws. Researcher Scott Masten and his colleagues, writing in the *Journal of the American Medical Association*, state:

> The amount learned during the GDL process may not be comparable to what was learned previously, when young drivers learned through experience alone. . . . Some important lessons of experience, such as the need for self-regulation and what it means to be fully responsible for a vehicle, cannot be learned until teens begin driving alone. Under GDL laws this now occurs at least 6 months later, reducing the time that young drivers have to learn before they turn 18.

Also, there has been speculation that additional supervision by parents may be counterproductive since teen drivers may have picked up their poor driving habits from their parents in the first place.

In discussing driving restrictions, the media often point out that motor vehicle accidents are the leading cause of death among teenagers. This statement is not particularly impressive on further reflection, however, because teens rarely get the diseases from which older people die, and few are exposed to other potentially dangerous situations, so such a ranking is unsurprising. A more meaningful statistic is that teens are much more likely to be involved in serious motor vehicle accidents than are older drivers. The reasons for this fact are controversial. Experts are divided as to whether it is inherent in being young or whether the amount of driving experience is what matters, regardless of age.

Some scientists say that the brains of teenagers are not fully mature and that they are therefore incapable of judging difficult driving situations. People who hold this view, or who merely think young teens have not had enough time to learn responsibility, sometimes argue that the minimum driving age should be eighteen, as it is in most European countries; however, those who believe safe driving depends on experience maintain that if the minimum driving age were raised, it would merely increase the age of the drivers most likely to cause accidents.

Although, statistically, young drivers are more likely to be dangerous drivers than are their elders, this is not true of all of them. Many teens are good drivers, who take seriously their obligation to handle a car safely. In the opinion of some people, it is unfair to restrict their driving privileges because of the irresponsible behavior of a minority, especially since the problem drivers are likely to ignore the restrictions anyway. Some also believe that if lack of supervised driving experience causes accidents, then GDL laws should apply to novice drivers of all ages rather than just to young teens. There is a reason for the distinction, however: Young people below age eighteen are minors, while those over eighteen are legally adults. Society has always restricted minors in ways adults are not on grounds of the need to protect youngsters. Driving is a privilege rather than a right, even for adults, but it is not surprising that the law requires minors to meet more stringent requirements in order to earn it.

The articles, personal narratives, and court opinions offered in *Teen Rights and Freedoms: Driving* explore various sides of this trending issue.

Chronology

1903   Massachusetts and Missouri become the first states to issue driver's licenses.

1908   Rhode Island becomes the first state to test driving skills before issuing a driver's license.

1909   Pennsylvania becomes the first state to specify a minimum age (eighteen) for those seeking a driver's license.

1911   Maine becomes the first state to specify sixteen as the minimum age for obtaining a driver's license.

1913   New Jersey becomes the first state to require a written test in addition to a driving test.

1920   Oregon becomes the first state to issue a learner's permit.

1954   South Dakota becomes the last state to require a driving test.

1968   North Dakota becomes the last state to specify a minimum age (fourteen) for obtaining a driver's license.

1982   The National Highway Traffic Safety Administration drops driver education as a priority, and federal funding for it is no longer available to high schools.

1996	Florida becomes the first state to enact a graduated driver licensing (GDL) law.
2001	New York becomes the first state to ban the use of handheld cell phones while driving.
2002	New Jersey becomes the first state to ban the use of wireless communication devices while driving by holders of a learner's permit or provisional license.
2007	Washington becomes the first state to ban texting while driving.
2010	A New Jersey state law goes into effect requiring teen drivers who have a learner's permit or provisional driver's license to display identifying decals on their cars.
2010	The Illinois Supreme Court, in *People v. Boeckmann*, rules that teens can lose their driver's license for underage drinking even if they were not driving.
2011	The Safe Teen and Novice Driver Uniform Protection (STANDUP) Act, which would provide for uniform GDL laws through the United States, is introduced in Congress but fails to pass.

2011   The *Journal of the American Medical Association* publishes the results of a study showing that while GDL laws have saved the lives of sixteen- and seventeen-year-olds, they have increased the number of fatal crashes among eighteen- and nineteen-year-old drivers.

2012   North Dakota becomes the last state to put a GDL law into effect.

> "Per mile driven, teen drivers ages 16
> to 19 are three times more likely than
> drivers aged 20 and older to be in a
> fatal crash."

Many Factors Lead to Unsafe Driving by Teens

Centers for Disease Control and Prevention

This viewpoint by the Centers for Disease Control and Prevention, a component of the US Department of Health and Human Services, states that motor vehicle crashes are the leading cause of death for US teens. In 2010, it asserts, 2,700 of them were killed and almost 282,000 were treated in emergency rooms due to traffic accidents. Inexperience, interacting with passengers, and engaging in unsafe practices such as speeding and reckless driving are among the factors that increase the risk, the author contends. Research has shown that such accidents can be reduced by graduated driver licensing (GDL) laws designed to ensure that teens will gain experience before being given full driving privileges.

Motor vehicle crashes are the leading cause of death for U.S. teens. In 2010, seven teens ages 16 to 19 died every day from motor vehicle injuries. Per mile driven, teen drivers ages 16 to 19 are three times more likely than drivers aged 20 and older

Centers for Disease Control and Prevention, "Teen Drivers: Fact Sheet," CDC.gov, October 2, 2012.

to be in a fatal crash. Fortunately, teen motor vehicle crashes are preventable, and proven strategies can improve the safety of young drivers on the road.

In 2010, about 2,700 teens in the United States aged 16–19 were killed and almost 282,000 were treated and released from emergency departments for injuries suffered in motor-vehicle crashes.

Young people ages 15–24 represent only 14% of the U.S. population. However, they account for 30% ($19 billion) of the total costs of motor vehicle injuries among males and 28% ($7 billion) of the total costs of motor vehicle injuries among females.

Who Is Most at Risk?

The risk of motor vehicle crashes is higher among 16- to 19-year-olds than among any other age group. In fact, per mile driven, teen drivers ages 16 to 19 are three times more likely than drivers aged 20 and older to be in a fatal crash.

Among teen drivers, those at especially high risk for motor vehicle crashes are:

- Males: In 2010, the motor vehicle death rate for male drivers and passengers ages 16 to 19 was almost two times that of their female counterparts.
- Teens driving with teen passengers: The presence of teen passengers increases the crash risk of unsupervised teen drivers. This risk increases with the number of teen passengers.
- Newly licensed teens: Crash risk is particularly high during the first months of licensure.

What Factors Put Teen Drivers at Risk?

- Teens are more likely than older drivers to underestimate dangerous situations or not be able to recognize hazardous situations.

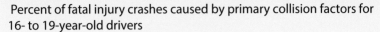

TEEN DRIVER CRASH STATISTICS

Percent of fatal injury crashes caused by primary collision factors for 16- to 19-year-old drivers

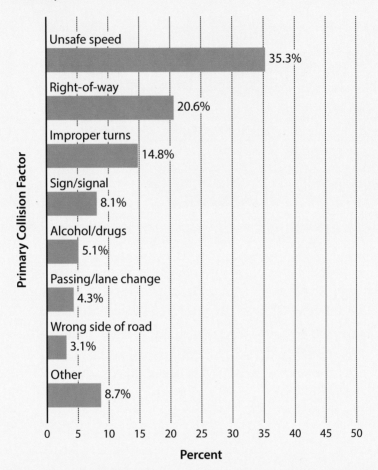

Taken from: "Young Drivers," California Department of Motor Vehicles, 2011. www.dmv.ca.gov.

- Teens are more likely than older drivers to speed and allow shorter headways (the distance from the front of one vehicle to the front of the next). The presence of male teenage passengers increases the likelihood of this risky driving behavior.

According to the Centers for Disease Control and Prevention, car accidents are the leading cause of death among teens. © Peter Dazeley/Photographer's Choice/Getty Images.

- Among male drivers between 15 and 20 years of age who were involved in fatal crashes in 2010, 39% were speeding at the time of the crash and 25% had been drinking.
- Compared with other age groups, teens have the lowest rate of seat belt use. In 2011, only 54% of high school students reported they always wear seat belts when riding with someone else.

At all levels of blood alcohol concentration (BAC), the risk of involvement in a motor vehicle crash is greater for teens than for older drivers.

In 2010, 22% of drivers aged 15 to 20 involved in fatal motor vehicle crashes were drinking.

- In a national survey conducted in 2011, 24% of teens reported that, within the previous month, they had ridden with a driver who had been drinking alcohol and 8% reported having driven after drinking alcohol within the same one-month period.

- In 2010, 56% of drivers aged 15 to 20 [who] were killed in motor vehicle crashes after drinking and driving were not wearing a seat belt.
- In 2010, half of teen deaths from motor vehicle crashes occurred between 3 PM and midnight and 55% occurred on Friday, Saturday, or Sunday.

How Can Deaths and Injuries Resulting from Crashes Involving Teen Drivers Be Prevented?

There are proven methods to helping teens become safer drivers. Research suggests that the most comprehensive graduated drivers licensing (GDL) programs are associated with reductions of 38% and 40% in fatal and injury crashes, respectively, among 16-year-old drivers.

Graduated driver licensing . . . systems are designed to delay full licensure while allowing teens to get their initial driving experience under low-risk conditions.

When parents know their state's GDL laws, they can help enforce the laws and, in effect, help keep their teen drivers safe.

"The selection of a particular licensing age ... reflects practices during the early history of driver licensing laws."

Age Restrictions for Obtaining a Driver's License Were Adopted Early in the Twentieth Century

Daniel R. Mayhew, Michele Fields, and Herbert M. Simpson

In this viewpoint Daniel R. Mayhew, senior vice president at the Traffic Industry Research Foundation, and fellow researchers Michele Fields and Herbert M. Simpson tell how age restrictions for obtaining a driver's license originated. Such restrictions, the authors assert, were first mentioned in state laws passed in 1909 and 1910. By 1937 only fifteen more states had adopted such laws, and the last one was not passed until 1954. At first, most states prohibited driving by people under age eighteen except when accompanied by a fully licensed driver. The introduction of child labor laws, however, which generally prohibited teens from working outside the home until the age of sixteen, led to this age becoming the most common minimum age for driving, although in agricultural states fourteen-year-olds were permitted to operate farm machinery. Age restrictions on driving also freed up the courts from having to decide on a case-by-case basis whether a driver was too young to drive in determining the liability for accidents. Although the choice of sixteen as the usual age of sufficient maturity was somewhat arbitrary, it was based on reasonable assumptions.

Since the advent of the motor vehicle at the beginning of the 20th century, driver's licenses were issued principally as sources of revenue and means to identify drivers who could be held responsible for damages inflicted by their motor vehicles on other people and/or property. The first driver's license is believed to have been issued in 1899 in Chicago, Illinois, to operate a steam-propelled vehicle.

However, laws governing driver's licenses did not emerge for another five years. The first states to introduce such laws were Massachusetts and Missouri in 1903. . . . It took five decades for licensing laws to be adopted in all jurisdictions. South Dakota was the last to do so in 1954.

Even in the early years of licensing laws, when revenue and driver identification were the principal focus, state authorities recognized that licenses could be used to ensure public safety. Indeed, the 1899 law in Chicago required "the Chief Health Officer to determine the applicant's ability to operate in a safe manner the vehicle amongst horse drawn vehicles on city streets." With rapid increases in motorization, concern about the mounting number of traffic crashes led to the realization that licensing procedures could be used to control drivers and, presumably, promote road safety. This perspective is reflected in very early state laws. For example, as early as 1906, in *Emerson Troy Granite Co. v. Pearson*, the Supreme Court of New Hampshire concluded that "The vehicles referred to in this chapter have recently come into use, and have introduced a new and serious peril to travelers upon highways. . . . Registration of them is required to enable persons to readily discover their character, and who owns or has control of them, so that in case any wrong is done in their use the responsibility for it can be easily ascertained. But registration is not full compliance with the statute; the person who operates a vehicle must be licensed. The object of the license is to furnish a further guaranty that proper use of the vehicle will be made, and that it will be operated in compliance with the law."

Since these early days, the protection of the public has continued to be a major rationale for driver's licenses; obtaining one requires a driver to meet certain minimum standards. At the same time, the emphasis on public safety has provided the authority for states to set the standards and regulations inherent in licensing: "In the interest of public safety and welfare the state, in the proper exercise of its police power, may make and enforce regulations reasonably calculated to promote proper care on the part of those who use the highways. This includes the power to require drivers of motor vehicles to be licensed and to prescribe the conditions under which the driving privilege may be granted and retained" ([R.L.] Donigan and [R.C.] Fisher).

Origins of Age Requirements

The earliest legislation determining who could and could not drive did not include both licensing and minimum age requirements. For example, the first operator's certificate for a person desiring to use a motor vehicle as a mechanic, employee, or for hire was introduced in New York State in 1903, but it was not until the Callan Law in 1910 that an age restriction was introduced. This law required that drivers be 18 or older or be accompanied by a licensed driver or owner of the vehicle.

Age restrictions also were absent in the 1903 law introduced in the Commonwealth of Pennsylvania to regulate the operation of motor vehicles. The first mention of an age restriction appears in Pennsylvania's 1909 licensing laws, which state, "No person under 18 years of age, whether the owner of a motor-vehicle or not, shall operate any motor-vehicle, without first obtaining from the State Highway Department a special license to do so. Such licenses shall

The Rise of Teen Car Culture

The most powerful influence on teenagers' relationships with cars has been American pop culture, which has always viewed cars as more than merely a means of transportation. . . .

The postwar boom of the 1950s spawned the teen car culture. As the economy once again surged—offering plenty of part-time jobs to students—teenagers could afford used cars of their own. And they made them a reflection of themselves.

"The ability to tune and soup-up muscle cars gave average Joes the opportunity to show off their power, their speed and their style in a way that personified the car as character," notes a history of the period.

Hollywood added another layer of meaning: Movies like *Rebel Without a Cause* (1955) made dragsters and motorcycles a form of anti-establishment defiance for alienated youth. The film's wild popularity among teenagers spawned imitators. . . .

Such movies typically played at drive-in theaters, which made cars symbolically important—as the place where teen dating often began.

Driving was, in a word, cool.

At the same time, teens seemed to identify with rock 'n' roll music as much as they did with their cars. Rock music and cars seemed made for each other in the 1950s. . . . And in cities and towns large and small across America, the songs could be heard blaring from teenagers' car radios.

William Triplett, "Teen Driving: Should States
Impose Tougher Restrictions?," CQ Researcher,
vol. 15, no. 1, January 7, 2005.

be granted only when the State Highway Commissioner is satisfied, after such tests or information as he may see fit to require, that the applicant is competent to operate a motor vehicle, and the granting or refusing of such an application shall be entirely within the discretion of the said Highway Commissioner." . . .

The very earliest driver licensing laws did not include age restrictions, and some of the early age restrictions were passed by states that had not yet enacted laws requiring all drivers to be licensed. Between 1910 and 1935, five states (Colorado, Illinois, Maine, New York, and Texas) passed minimum age laws before passing mandatory licensing laws for noncommercial drivers. When minimum age laws first were introduced, it is noteworthy that some restricted driving to people 18 and older unless they were accompanied by a licensed driver or owner of the vehicle (in New York) or obtained a special license to drive (in Pennsylvania).

These age requirements were not changed for more than a decade; the licensing age remained 18 from about 1910 until the early 1920s in Connecticut and the late 1920s in New York. Connecticut modified its laws in 1921 to allow any person 16 or older to obtain a license and drive while under the instruction of, and accompanied by, a licensed operator. And in 1929 New York State introduced a law that gave "junior operator" status to 16 and 17 years-olds, allowing them to drive to and from school or work but not in New York City. . . .

From 1919 to 1937, 15 states, none of them urbanized, passed minimum licensing age laws; among these, 9 permitted driving at age 16, 4 at age 15, and 2 at age 14. It is possible that predominantly rural states would choose a younger minimum licensing age than more urbanized states. . . .

Rationale for Minimum Licensing Age Laws

Although concern for public welfare was a major factor in the adoption of minimum licensing age requirements, so was concern for the welfare of adolescents. Such concern emerged from a change in social attitudes toward childhood and adolescence around the beginning of the 20th century. As observed by [F.R.] Marks, "social upheaval that accompanied the burgeoning industrialization of the time gave rise to profound changes in the way in which children were seen in reference to both their parents and the world." This trend at the time was best exemplified by the implementation of three major institutional changes: the juvenile court system, the prohibition of child labor, and compulsory education. As a consequence of this trend, many activities became regulated by age, arguably the most important of which was the age at which children could begin working.

Child labor laws were enacted during this period and undoubtedly influenced other social legislation, including licensing age, that affected minors. . . .

Child labor laws also commonly regulated employment-related driving, establishing 16 as the minimum age at which workers could operate trucks and other vehicles. . . .

Child labor laws established minimum ages for children to work, typically providing that children younger than 14 may not work, and when and in what businesses children ages 14–16 and 16–18 may work. There are, however, numerous exceptions; the most noteworthy for this study is the exception for agricultural work. . . .

Although lawmakers recognized the need to safeguard the welfare of adolescents, in the early years of driver licensing laws a consensus failed to emerge as to the optimum age for licensing. . . . At issue in these early years was whether a specific age— e.g., 16 or 18—was a "reasonable" choice for a minimum licensing age.

By the mid-to-late 1920s, however, the need for uniformity in the control and regulation of drivers emerged as a critical issue in the United States. In this regard, the first Uniform Vehicle Code in 1926 recommended that the minimum age for an operator's license be set at 16. This guideline, and the fact that some states already had a minimum licensing age of 16, influenced other states to follow suit. Some degree of uniformity was achieved, but the choice of 16 appears to reflect a compromise between safety and mobility. It is not a surprising compromise, given that child labor laws permitted employment at age 16 often in hazardous occupations, that agricultural work was permitted by children of virtually any age, and that farming necessitated the use of heavy equipment and trucks.

Even though licensing authorities maintained that people younger than a prescribed age were, as a class, immature and lacking in judgment and therefore a threat to public welfare, many felt there were reasons to allow teenagers to drive. This was especially the case in rural, agricultural states that allowed adolescents as young as 14 to operate motor vehicles. An older minimum licensing age would have been unacceptable where adolescents were expected to work on farms.

However, because people younger than 16 are minors in most states, several safeguards have been introduced to ensure that immature and unqualified adolescents are not allowed the same access to licenses as adults. For example, parents are required to sign for their 16- and 17-year-olds, thereby assuming financial responsibility in the event of a crash. Parents also can revoke their permission, thus suspending or canceling the teenager's license. Other measures that were introduced include a learner's period to allow young people an opportunity to practice driving under supervision, driver education and training as a prerequisite to obtaining a license before age 18, and a road test to assess young people's driving skills prior to granting them licenses. . . .

The Public Welfare

As the use of motor vehicles became popular in the early 1900s, public authorities began to recognize the need to control the emerging problem of traffic collisions and congestion. This is not surprising considering that the number of motor vehicles was rapidly increasing at that time—from only 8,000 registered vehicles in 1900 to 468,500 in 1910 and more than 9 million by 1920.

Coincident with the rise in motorization was an increase in the number of crashes, injuries, and deaths. For example, deaths numbered only 400 in 1907, compared with 1,900 in 1910 and

12,500 in 1920. Unfortunately, the rapid proliferation of the automobile as a popular means of transportation and the accompanying rise in crashes left lawmakers far behind.

The driver's license and, more importantly, the licensing process was seen as a means to control the operation of motor vehicles and to protect the public welfare. Not surprisingly, as the disproportionate involvement of young people in road crashes came to the public's attention, lawmakers began legislating age requirements.

Indeed, the safety objectives of driver licensing and, more specifically, age requirements have long been recognized by the courts. In a personal injury case caused by an unlicensed 16-year-old, a New York court noted: "The object and purpose of the [licensing] statute is to promote the safety of those traveling the public highways. While a motor vehicle is not, in and of itself, to be deemed a dangerous machine, nevertheless it becomes such in the hands of a careless and inexperienced person. The statute has, in effect, so declared when it forbids its operation by persons

Since the dawn of the automobile, driver's licenses have been issued to drivers before they are legally allowed to drive. © Driver's License/Alamy.

under the age of 18. It . . . declares that such persons do not possess the requisite care and judgment to run motor vehicles on the public highways without endangering the lives and limbs of others" (*Schulz v. Morrison*, 1915). . . .

It is, however, puzzling that it took several decades for some jurisdictions to recognize the threat posed by young drivers and then take appropriate action. For example, it is unlikely that a problem existed with young drivers in New York State, one of the first jurisdictions to adopt a minimum age in the early 1900s, but not South Dakota, where an age requirement was delayed until the 1960s. . . .

Although no documentation was found indicating that liability concerns prompted the establishment of licensing requirements and minimum licensing age laws, it is clear that their existence was a benefit for courts. As vehicles became commonplace and young people started driving, liability issues inevitably arose. In the absence of a legislative determination of minimum age, it would be left to the courts to decide, on a case-by-case basis, the age at which people are presumed to be too young to drive and therefore the age at which it would be negligent to allow them to drive. Minimum licensing age laws relieved courts of this burden and established statewide consistency on the issue. Several of the early cases in which the legislative intent of minimum age laws was addressed were personal injury cases. The opinions made it clear that the question of a minimum licensing age was best left to the legislature, not the courts. . . .

When minimum ages were questioned, courts reviewed the statutory minimum ages to see if the ages the legislatures chose were rationally based. Courts sustained minimum licensing ages as a rational response to a common understanding that children would make poor drivers. For example, according to the Supreme Court of New Hampshire, "A minor, in the absence of evidence to the contrary, is universally considered to be lacking in judgement. His normal condition is one of recognized incompetency" (*Charbonneau v. MacRury*). According to this decision, adolescents lack judgement and are therefore by statute incompetent. . . .

The selection of 16 or 18 as the age for determining incompetence and immaturity was not based on any definitive scientific evidence. Indeed, the courts have recognized that the stage at which someone reaches physical and mental maturity varies among individuals and that a variety of factors including "teaching and experience" account for these differences. As observed by the Supreme Court of New Hampshire, "it follows that the age at which maturity is in fact reached cannot be determined with mathematical accuracy. The necessities of society, however, require that some age should be considered as prima facie evidence of maturity" (*Charbonneau v. MacRury*). Similarly, in an early Nebraska case the Supreme Court stated: "The question is whether the classification is reasonable. It is quite possible that some persons under the age of 16 years are more apt . . . than many adults, but the fact remains that, as a class, they have not, at that age, attained the discretion and judgment which would make it safe for them to operate motor vehicles upon the highway. The line must be drawn somewhere, and the only question is whether the Legislature acted arbitrarily or reasonably in drawing the line at 16 years of age" (*State ex rel. Oleson v. Graunke*).

Most states draw the line at 16 because they believe it is "reasonable" to assume persons younger than this age are, as a class, not mature enough to be given the responsibility of operating a motor vehicle. Other states have selected 14 or 18 as the age at which someone may drive.

The preceding discussion suggests that the selection of a particular licensing age has been somewhat arbitrary but not capricious; it was based on a reasonable assessment of the age at which someone is mature enough to drive. Certainly, this reflects practices during the early history of driver licensing laws.

| "Graduated licensing programs . . .
dramatically reduce the rate of teen
driver fatal crashes."

Graduated Driver Licensing Laws Reduce Fatal Teen Crashes

National Institutes of Health

Three studies funded by the National Institutes of Health, a US government medical research agency, found that graduated driver licensing (GDL) laws reduced fatal crashes by up to 14 percent among sixteen- to seventeen-year-olds. These laws require that teens get practice in driving before receiving a full license, not only with a learner's permit but for a specified period after passing a driving test. The greatest decrease in fatal crashes occurred in states whose GDL laws also included other provisions, such as limits on the number of teen passengers or restrictions on driving at night. The laws were less effective in preventing crashes due to speeding than those related to teen drinking.

Programs that grant privileges to new drivers in phases—known as graduated licensing programs—dramatically re-

National Institutes of Health, "Graduated Drivers Licensing Programs Reduce Fatal Teen Crashes," *NIH News*, November 4, 2011.

duce the rate of teen driver fatal crashes, according to three studies funded by the National Institutes of Health [NIH].

Such graduated licensing laws were adopted by all 50 states and the District of Columbia between 1996 and 2011. The NIH-supported research effort shows that such programs reduced the rate of fatal crashes among 16- to 17-year-olds by 8 to 14 percent.

Reductions in fatal crashes were greatest in states that had enacted other restrictions on young drivers. The greatest reductions in young driver crashes were seen in states that had adopted graduated driver licensing laws in combination with mandatory seat belt laws or laws requiring a loss of the driver's license as a penalty for possession or use of alcohol by youth aged 20 or younger.

In addition, limiting driving at night or with teenaged passengers, in combination with graduated licensing laws, had greater reductions in overall crash rates involving teen drivers than graduated licensing laws alone.

Graduated licensing programs generally require new drivers to complete three phases before they receive their license. The first stage involves issuing a learner's permit, in which the new driver must practice driving with a licensed driver aged 21 or older. The second stage allows driving, but only under certain conditions—for example, not late at night, and without teen passengers in the car. After completing these phases, the driver receives a full license—in some states, after reaching age 18.

Effect of GDL Laws Varies

One of the studies, an analysis of 15- to 17-year-old drivers killed in crashes between 1999 and 2008, concluded that the effect of these laws did not appear to be uniform across racial and ethnic groups. The laws did not appear to reduce fatalities among Hispanic teen drivers, although they did have an effect among white, African-American and Asian teenagers.

"Everyone hoped that that graduated driver licensing would help to protect new drivers, but it was necessary to evaluate whether the new laws did indeed have their desired effects," said Rebecca L. Clark, Ph.D., chief of the Demographic and Behavioral Sciences branch of the NIH's Eunice Kennedy Shriver National Institute of Child Health and Human Development (NICHD), which funded the studies. "These studies not only confirm the effectiveness of graduated licensing approach, they also identify additional protective factors."

The studies were conducted by James C. Fell and colleagues at the Pacific Institute for Research and Evaluation (PIRE) in Calverton, Md. Fell was the first author on a study analyzing [the] effect of graduated licensing laws in the United States, which he undertook with PIRE colleagues Kristina Jones, Eduardo Romano, Ph.D., and Robert Voas, Ph.D. Their findings appear in *Traffic Injury Prevention*. In a study published in the *Journal of Safety Research*, Fell, Michael Todd, and Dr. Voas looked at the effects of licensing restrictions in the graduated driver licensing laws. Dr. Romano, Fell and Dr. Voas collaborated on the study of race and ethnicity and graduated licensing laws, which appears in the *Annals of Advances in Automotive Medicine*.

For all three studies, the researchers analyzed data from a national database of information about fatal crashes maintained by the National Highway Traffic Safety Administration.

Using data from 1990 to 2007, the researchers compared the rate of fatal crashes among two groups of drivers: 16- and 17-year-olds and 21- to 25-year-olds. They then tracked how this ratio changed after graduated licensing laws were adopted in each state. Their analysis showed that characteristics of a state's licensing law influenced the law's effectiveness. The most effective legislation had at least five of seven key elements:

1. A minimum age of 16 for a learner's permit
2. A mandatory waiting period of at least six months before a driver with a learner's permit can apply for a provisional license
3. A requirement for 50 to 100 hours of supervised driving

4. A minimum age of 17 for a provisional license
5. Restrictions on driving at night
6. A limit on the number of teenage passengers allowed in the car
7. A minimum age of 18 for a full license

Nighttime Driving Restrictions Increase Laws' Effectiveness

The researchers also looked at the effect of nighttime and passenger restrictions on fatal crash rates. As a result of their analysis, they estimated that laws restricting driving at night reduced fatal crashes at night among 16- and 17-year-old drivers by 10 percent in comparison to states that did not have nighttime driving restrictions. Nighttime restrictions also reduced involvement in nighttime crashes among 16- and 17-year-old drinking drivers

In some states, limited licenses prohibit teens from driving at night, which studies have shown reduces fatal accidents. © Golden Pixels LLC/Alamy.

The Impact of Stronger Graduated Driving Laws

- According to the Automobile Club of Southern California, teenage passenger deaths and injuries resulting from crashes involving 16-year-old drivers declined by 40 percent from 1998 to 2000, the first three years of California's graduated driver licensing program. The number of at-fault collisions involving 16-year-old drivers decreased by 24 percent during the same period.

- In 1997, the first full year of its graduated driver licensing system, Florida experienced a nine percent reduction in fatal and injurious crashes among teenage drivers between the ages of 15 and 18, compared with 1995, according to the Insurance Institute for Highway Safety.

- The *Journal of the American Medical Association* reports that crashes involving 16-year-old drivers decreased between 1995 and 1999 by 25 percent in Michigan and 27 percent in North Carolina. Comprehensive graduated driver licensing systems were implemented in 1997 in these States.

Tim Bishop, "The STANDUP Act," Congressman Tim Bishop website, US House of Representatives, 2009. http://timbishop.house.gov.

by an estimated 13 percent. Laws that established a midnight curfew for provisional drivers appeared to be most effective at reducing nighttime crashes, the researchers concluded. In addition, laws restricting the number of teen passengers in a car driven by a 16- or 17-year-old appeared to reduce fatal crashes with teen passengers by 9 percent.

"States have followed a variety of approaches to their legislation about graduated driver licensing laws," said Fell. "These findings on nighttime and passenger restrictions might be useful to states wishing to make their graduated licensing programs more effective."

In a separate analysis, the researchers compared data from the years in which individual states had these laws in effect to the total sample, spanning the period from 1999 to 2008. In addition, the researchers evaluated crashes in which speed or alcohol was a contributing factor.

The researchers found that the rate of 15- to 17-year-old drivers killed in single vehicle crashes dropped after states adopted graduated licensing laws. In particular, they concluded that these laws were more effective at reducing alcohol-related fatalities than those in which speed was a factor.

"GDL laws . . . were associated with an
increase of 2724 fatalities from fatal
crash involvements of 18 year old
drivers."

Graduated Driver Licensing Laws Increase Fatal Crashes for Eighteen-Year-Olds

James C. Fell and Eduardo Romano

Authors James C. Fell and Eduardo Romano conducted statistical research to determine the effectiveness of graduated driver licensing (GDL) laws in preventing fatal teen crashes. Since previous research had shown that such laws reduced crashes among sixteen-year-olds but increased them among eighteen-year-olds, the authors calculated the effect on each age separately. They also separated the groups by differing types of GDL laws. The study showed that restrictive GDL laws caused more lives to be lost among older teens than were saved among younger teens. It was suggested that this might have been because teens were delaying getting their licenses to avoid the requirements imposed by GDL laws or because teens who did gain driving experience in restricted situations were later exposed to riskier ones. Fell and Romano are researchers at the Pacific Institute for Research and Evaluation in Calverton, Maryland.

James C. Fell and Eduardo Romano, "Are Strong Graduated Driver Licensing Laws Having Unintended Consequences?," *US National Library of Medicine*, vol. 57, September 2013, pp. 351–352.

Motor-vehicle crashes are the leading cause of death for young people aged 15 to 20 in the United States, accounting for approximately 36% of their deaths. Graduated Driver Licensing (GDL) systems have been developed as an entry-level licensing program in the United States that gives young beginning drivers more time to learn the complex skills required to drive a motor vehicle. Typically, GDL programs require a supervised learning stage of 6 months or more, followed by an intermediate or provisional license stage of at least several months with restrictions on high-risk driving before a driver "graduates" to full license privileges with no restrictions (third stage). GDL laws now exist in all 50 States and the District of Columbia.

A recent study of GDL laws that appeared in the *Journal of the American Medical Association* (*JAMA*) found substantial reductions in fatal crashes of 16 year old drivers associated with the adoption of strong GDL laws (down 26%), but found increases in fatal crashes for 18 year olds in those same States (up 12%). The authors of this *JAMA* study suggested that strong GDL laws may

Graduated driver licensing laws have been shown in some cases to reduce significantly the number of fatal accidents among teenage drivers. © Ariel Skelley/The Image Bank/Getty Images.

have delayed licensure of many youth until they were 18 years old in order to avoid all the GDL provisions and requirements.

[Our objective was to] determine the effects of strong graduated driver licensing laws on the fatal crashes of young drivers separately aged 15, 16, 17, 18, 19 and 20 using a different, but appropriate, methodology compared to [the *JAMA* study].

Methods Used for the Study

We used a longitudinal panel cross-sectional time-series approach where we examined annual Fatality Analysis Reporting System (FARS) data for all 50 states and the District of Columbia from 1990 through 2007. We applied a Box and Jenkins ARIMA (Autoregressive Integrated Moving Average) intervention regression method [a statistical process] to evaluate the enactment of a GDL law (the intervention) on the fatal crash incidence among 15, 16, 17, 18, 19, and 20-year-old drivers. To account for crash exposure, we computed and compared ratios of the 15 to 20-year-old drivers involved in fatal crashes with one older age group: 21 to 25-year-old drivers. By using the crash population of 21- to 25-year-olds as proxy denominators for the 15–20-year-olds, we believe we controlled for most of the driving exposure elements common to both groups.

The Insurance Institute for Highway Safety (IIHS) rated a GDL law as good if it had five or more of the following seven components: (1) minimum age for a learner's permit; (2) mandatory waiting period before applying for intermediate license; (3) minimum hours of supervised driving; (4) minimum age for intermediate license; (5) nighttime restriction; (6) passenger limitation; and (7) minimum age for full licensing. Regression models for each age-group ratio were separately performed for the three categories of GDL laws ("average," "good," and "less than good"). The ratios of interest (drivers aged 15, 16, 17, 18, 19, and 20 years old involved in fatal crashes relative to drivers aged 21–25 involved in fatal crashes) were then regressed on the GDL laws alone, with each of four potentially confounding

TEEN DRIVERS IN FATAL MOTOR VEHICLE CRASHES BEFORE AND AFTER GDL LAWS

Age Range	Period	Crashes	Rate (per 1,000 population)
16–17	Prelaw	506	18.5
	Postlaw	790	15.5
18–19	Prelaw	1,384	30.2
	Postlaw	1,092	34.9

Notes:
Prelaw years by age: 16 = 1/95–6/97; 17 = 1/95–6/98; 18 = 1/95–6/99; 19 = 1/95–6/00.
Transition period by age: 16 = 7/97–6/99; 17 = 7/98–6/00; 18 = 7/99–6/01; 19 = 7/00–6/02.
Postlaw years by age: 16 = 7/99–12/04; 17 = 7/00–12/04; 18 = 7/01–12/04; 19 = 7/02–12/04.

Taken from: Mike Males, "California's Graduated Driver License Law: Effects on Older Teenagers," *Californian Journal of Health Promotion*, vol. 4, no. 3, 2006, pp. 207–221. www.cjhp.org.

laws that could affect young drivers individually (e.g. zero tolerance laws, use and lose [loss of license for underage alcohol use], .08 BAC [blood alcohol concentration] laws, and primary seat belt laws), and with all four covariates included in the analysis. Implementation dates for GDL laws and their strength (good, fair, marginal, poor) were obtained from the IIHS. Outcome measures were the involvements in fatal crashes of 15, 16, 17, 18, 19 and 20 year old drivers as extracted from the Fatality Analysis Reporting System (FARS) developed and maintained by the National Highway Traffic Safety Administration (NHTSA).

Results of the Study

Using only the findings for each age that were significant (p<.05), 1945 lives were saved associated with GDL laws in general by the reductions in fatal crashes involving 16 year old drivers. For the "Good" GDL laws, there was a net increase in fatalities of 377 due to the increase in fatal crashes by 18 year old drivers, with an additional increase of 855 fatalities for the 19 year old drivers. "Good" GDL laws resulted in 2347 lives saved due to the reduction of 16 year old drivers in fatal crashes, but were associated with an increase of 2724 fatalities from fatal crash involvements of 18 year old drivers.

These results indicate that some of the lives of 15–17 year old novice drivers that the GDL save are offset among the associated increases in fatal crashes by 18–19 year old drivers. The reasons for such a finding of the GDL effects are unclear. They could be due to (1) novice 18–19 year olds beginning to drive without the protective framework of a GDL program by delaying licensure in the Good GDL states; (2) increased risk-taking behaviors by 18 and 19 year old drivers (e.g. impaired driving, late night driving, driving with teen passengers, lack of safety belt use, distracted driving); and/or (3) lack of experience to risky situations by 18–19 year old drivers in the Good GDL states because of the protective stages when they were 16 and 17 years old (e.g. late night driving; driving on high speed roads). Further research to clarify this finding is needed.

"If politicians really believed . . . that GDL's made drivers safer, they would require GDL licenses for all new drivers regardless of age."

Graduated Driver Licensing Laws Are Unfair and Endanger Lives

Bill Bystricky

In the following viewpoint Bill Bystricky argues that graduated driver licensing (GDL) laws endanger lives because it has been found that they increase traffic fatalities among eighteen- and nineteen-year-olds. People who favor these laws claim that they want to keep young people safe, he notes, when actually what they want is to keep younger teens from driving at all. In his opinion they are motivated only by ageism and the desire to keep teens powerless; if the real aim of GDL laws were to increase safety, they would apply to all *new drivers, not just to teens, Bystricky argues. Moreover, the proposal to establish national GDL standards restricts cell phone use while driving only for teens, whereas cell phone use is equally dangerous—and more common—among adults. Bystricky, who formerly wrote under the pen name Bill Medic, owns the website Pro-Youth Pages, which advocates more rights for teens.*

In America, it used to be that when you were learning to drive, you were issued a learner's permit allowing you to drive with supervision; then after you proved to the Department of Motor Vehicles (DMV) that you could drive safely, you were issued a driver license giving you the full right to drive on America's highways.

That's still true for adults learning to drive. But for America's teenagers, some politicians are changing the rules. Some states have now instituted "graduated driver license programs" (GDL's), and a new proposal in Congress would force all states to adopt this policy.

In these states, a teenager is not even allowed to prove herself to the DMV until she has spent many, many hours driving with her parents, regardless of whether those parents are good drivers or bad. If her parent is a bad driver who pushes the wrong habits on her, that's just her tough luck. Then, if she can still pass the DMV test, she is given, not a full license, but a second-class license that allows her drive only under certain circumstances.

These GDL laws not only insult youth, they endanger lives.

Graduated Driving Laws Do Not Improve Safety

Backers of GDL laws claim they are motivated, not by ageism, but by love. They say they want teenagers to be safe, and these restrictions will keep teenagers driving safely.

But studies have shown just the opposite is true. The *Californian Journal of Health Promotion* published a 2006 study that found:

> 18- and 19-year-olds subjected to GDL programs experienced net increases of 11% in traffic fatalities and 10% in involvements of drivers in fatal accidents, more than offsetting the declines among younger teenagers.

In other words, the study found that:
1. There were declines in fatalities among those younger than

18—but only because fewer were now driving at all. These GDL licenses bore so many restrictions they were nearly worthless.

2. Older teenagers who had gone through the GDL program were significantly *more likely* to cause accidents than teenagers who had been driving with full licenses all along. That's not surprising since teenagers under GDL were less able to stay in practice after proving themselves to the DMV.

3. Overall, the number of deaths caused by GDL was larger than the number of deaths prevented by it.

Rather than saving lives, these GDL policies are killing people. Why do politicians want to spread this problem nationwide?

Graduated Driving Laws Are Ageist

Clearly, their motivation is not safety. If politicians really believed, for whatever reason, that GDL's made drivers safer, they

The Department of Motor Vehicles, such as this one in Hawaii, is the gateway for teen drivers to freedom on the road. © David L. Moore/Alamy.

Graduated Driving Laws May Increase Deaths Among Teen Drivers

The increase in fatal accidents involving unlicensed teenaged drivers of all ages suggests a main effect of California's GDL [graduated driver licensing] law has been to deter some of the postlaw population from obtaining driver's licenses at all. The increase in accidents by unlicensed teenage drivers after the law took effect does not reflect a larger trend. . . . However, 18–19-year-old drivers lawfully licensed under the GDL program also show increased fatal crash risks.

The second alternative hypothesis is that GDL programs are an inefficient means of reducing young-driver risks because they target all teenagers rather than the specific high-risk fraction responsible for most serious accidents, and because their major element of teenage driver training (supervision by parents or other nearby adults) may add to rather than reduce risks in that problematic fraction. Despite recent suggestions in the press of extreme teenage risks, traffic fatalities caused by teenaged drivers are rare events, averaging approximately one fatality per four million trips by 16–17-year-old drivers, or per 15 million miles driven by teens. Given that the best predictor of a teenagers' driving record is their parents' driving record, GDL laws deputizing any parent or nearby adult over age 25 with a license as a driving instructor for novice teenagers may work to perpetuate intergenerational bad driving habits.

The results of this study add to previously expressed concerns that GDL laws, especially restrictive ones, have negative effects on older teenaged drivers, particularly males. This potential merits reassessment of the advisability and structure of policies designed to delay adult privileges and greater caution in recommending such policies until longer-term effects on both younger and older teenagers and young adults can be quantified.

Mike Males, "California's Graduated Driver License Law: Effects on Older Teenagers," Californian Journal of Health Promotion, *vol. 4, no. 3, 2006, pp. 207–221. www.cjhp.org.*

would require GDL licenses for all new drivers regardless of age. Instead they target the one group that cannot fight back at the ballot box.

We must conclude GDL-supporters want, not safer driving, but less driving by teenagers. These politicians have the same motive as leaders in Saudi Arabia who ban women from driving. They want to make American teenagers even more dependent, even more powerless, even more humiliated.

These politicians will pander to ageist voters even if it means they have to sweep under the rug a few more highway deaths.

The STANDUP Act Unfairly Targets Younger Drivers

The STANDUP [Safe Teen And Novice Driver Uniform Protection] Act now [as of 2010] making its way through Congress would impose these deadly GDL's on every state in the union.

Adding insult to injury, the bill would also ban drivers younger than 18—and only drivers younger than 18—from using cell phones or texting while driving. This is especially insulting because studies have now proven not only that these activities are dangerous for all drivers, but that drivers younger than 18 are the ones least likely to be guilty.

A recent study by the Pew Research Center found that ¾ of all adults who own cell phones have talked on the phone while driving, but only ½ of such teenagers have. The study also found that 47% of adults who text have done so while driving, but only 34% of such teenagers have. Far from the stereotype of teenaged risk-takers, in the real world, it is adults who are most likely to engage in this risky behavior.

Since teenagers are the ones least likely to do these reckless acts, targeting teenagers with this ban makes no sense from a safety standpoint. It is an ageist insult.

NYRA [National Youth Rights Association]'s Executive Director, Alex Koroknay-Palicz, offers another interesting point on this issue:

[R]esearch shows that a teen on a cell phone has the same reaction times as a senior citizen not on a cell phone. If we believe teens on cell phones are so dangerous that federal legislation is needed, shouldn't we, by the same token, ban all drivers over 65? The reality is that texting or talking on a cell phone is dangerous for all drivers. Some research even concludes it is comparable to drunk driving. Can you imagine having a law that says drunk driving is just fine as long as you are over 18?

Ban drivers older than 65? Just because they're as dangerous as teenagers on cell phones? Our politicians will never allow that.

It is wrong to impose hardships on someone simply because of when she was born. But that is not why the elderly are protected. In California, after an elderly driver killed 10 people and injured more than 40, a few politicians suggested a new policy: elderly drivers, in order to renew their licenses, would be required to pass a behind-the-wheel DMV test—the same test teenagers in California have to pass to get their nearly worthless GDL licenses. That proposal didn't pass. It didn't even come close.

The elderly are allowed the vote, and they will not allow their freedom, their mobility, or their dignity to be threatened. The mobility of even the most dangerous adult is sacred, politicians therefore tell us, but the mobility of even the safest teenager is expendable. Young people (denied the right to vote, file lawsuits, or control money) are down, so politicians feel safe kicking them.

Politicians need to hear from us. They need to know we won't sit by and watch them kick youth again.

Editor's Note:

The STANDUP Act was introduced in Congress twice, in 2010 and 2011. It did not pass either time.

"Parents and teen drivers have sharply different views on how well [GDL] restrictions are being enforced."

Teens, Parents Differ on Graduated Driver's Licenses

Larry Copeland

In the following viewpoint Larry Copeland explains that graduated driver licensing (GDL) laws can work only if both teens and parents are committed to observing them. Yet according to a recent insurance company survey, there is a wide gap between teens' and parents' beliefs about how they are being enforced. For instance, 65 percent of parents say they monitor whether the rules regarding the number of passengers a teen may drive with are being followed by their teen drivers, but only 27 percent of teens agree that their parents monitor them. Some experts believe that parents are tolerating violations because they want teens to be able to drive themselves instead of having to take them everywhere. Copeland is a writer for USA Today.

Graduated Driver Licensing programs, in which young drivers earn privileges as they gain experience under the watchful eye of their parents, have become a crucial part of the nation's effort to ease teenagers through those dangerous first years of driving.

Every state has a GDL law, and experts agree that the best ones require buy-in from teen and parent to ensure that critical restrictions on such things as nighttime driving, teen passengers and texting are enforced.

But a new survey released by insurer State Farm indicates that parents and teen drivers have sharply different views of how well those restrictions are being enforced, which could be undercutting the programs' effectiveness.

For example, 87% of parents believe teens will obey GDL restrictions because of parental monitoring, but just 56% of teens say they're likely to do so.

"It's okay if I text behind the wheel. I have an app that drives the car."

© Randy Glasbergen/glasbergen.com.

When it comes to nighttime restrictions, which are designed to keep teens off the roads during riskier periods, 66% of parents say they almost always monitor whether their teens are obeying the rules; only 32% of teens say that's the case.

The findings are from an online survey in June [2013] of 500 parents of 14- to 17-year-old teen drivers, and 500 teen drivers age 14 to 17.

The parent-teen disconnect is even more jarring on passenger restrictions. The crash risk doubles for a teen driver with two young passengers and quadruples with three or more young passengers if no older passengers are in the vehicle, according to 2012 research by the AAA Foundation for Traffic Safety. Yet in the new survey, just 27% of teens said their parents usually keep track of whether they are following the rule on passengers, compared with 65% of parents who said they monitor.

Some experts say the survey might highlight an element of willful denial among some parents. In most GDL programs, teens are required to get at least 30 hours of parent-supervised

In many graduated driver licensing programs, supervised driving with a parent is a prerequisite to driving alone. © Gary S. Chapman/Photograher's Choice/Getty Images.

practice; then they move into the intermediate, provisional licensing stage, when they can drive alone but the nighttime and passenger restrictions apply. That is the riskiest time for novice drivers, but weary parents often pull back.

"Parents have been taxicab drivers for over 16 years," says Capt. Tom Didone of the Montgomery County, Md., Police Department. "They look at (provisional licensing) as an opportunity to allow their kids independence, to make their life easy. Parents don't understand that this can happen to them." His 15-year-old son, Ryan Thomas Didone, was killed in 2008 after getting into a car with several other teens and an inexperienced teen driver.

Some teens might be misleading parents by leaving home with one or no passengers and then picking up other teens, whose parents are also in the dark, says Sharon Baker, 53, of Seville, Ohio. "You have to build that trust with your kids," says Baker, an advocate for strong GDL laws since her only child, daughter Kelli, 17, was killed in a 2011 crash.

It's important for parents to actually monitor teen drivers, to regularly discuss the GDL rules and to establish clear consequences for violations, says Raygan Sylvester, 17, a senior at North Little Rock, Ark., High School. She's a cop's daughter and says: "If I get caught with more than one person in the car, my car will be taken away for a certain amount of time. If I got caught texting, I would definitely get my keys taken away and probably my phone taken away."

Parents and teens have different opinions on why some young drivers don't follow GDL rules. Parents think peer pressure is the biggest motivator for those who ignore the restrictions; teens say the most likely reason is their belief that they won't get a ticket.

Chief Chris Wagner of the Denville, N.J., Police Department says the teens' view reflects their sense of invulnerability but also shows the need for police to enforce GDL laws. "If a police officer pulls over a teen driver at night with four teenagers in the car and then lets them go with a warning, that's akin to letting a drunk driver drive down the road with a warning," he says.

There was one encouraging finding in the State Farm survey. The national focus on distracted driving is paying off: 82% of parents believe their teens are obeying bans on texting while driving; 72% of teens say that they are—a higher compliance rate than for any other GDL provision.

Chris Mullen, State Farm's director of technology research, says the survey can help experts establish effective GDL programs. "This is not an evaluation of GDL," she says. "This is an evaluation of awareness. It looks like parents and teens are disconnected. So we should be asking the question, 'Do we talk enough?'"

> *"Kyleigh's Law, which requires young
> drivers to display red decals on their
> vehicles to alert police to their age
> and driver's license status, has been
> controversial from its start in 2010."*

Requiring Teen Drivers to Display License Plate Decals Is Controversial

Courier News *(Somerville, NJ)*

*The following viewpoint discusses a report on the effectiveness
of Kyleigh's Law, a controversial New Jersey statute that requires
teen drivers with graduated driver license (GDL) restrictions to
display red decals on their vehicles' license plates to alert police of
their driver status. Many parents have objected to the law on the
grounds that the decals might attract predators and have tried to
get it repealed; some have even encouraged their children to remove them. A study found that after the law took effect, however,
the teen crash rate decreased, but the number of GDL violations
increased, which was interpreted to mean that the decals save lives.
The viewpoint suggests that while there may be other reasons for
the reduced number of crashes, if the law saves even a few lives,
opposition to it should be reconsidered. The* Courier News *is a central New Jersey newspaper based in Somerville.*

Kyleigh's Law, which requires young drivers to display red decals on their vehicles to alert police to their age and driver's license status, has been controversial from its start in 2010.

While the underlying goal of trying to prevent accidents involving teen drivers is laudable, critics have been plentiful, fearing the decals would expose young people to predators or police abuse. Lawmakers have even sought to overturn the measure, or at least its decal provision. Now comes some evidence that is supposed to show that the law is working and should remain intact. But the results of that study are quickly becoming as much an object of dispute as the decals themselves.

In a report published Tuesday [October 23, 2012] in the *American Journal of Preventative Medicine*, conducted by four researchers from Children's Hospital of Philadelphia, the crash rate for teen drivers was found to have decreased 9 percent when comparing crashes before and after the implementation of Kyleigh's Law on May 1, 2010.

A red decal is placed on a license plate during a ceremony in Trenton, New Jersey, to implement Kyleigh's Law, which requires drivers under twenty-one to display this decal. © AP Images/ Doug Hood.

The law, named for Kyleigh D'Alessio, a Long Valley teen killed in a 2006 crash, also requires a driver with a GDL, or graduated driver's license, to adhere to curfews, limits how many other teens can be in the vehicle as passengers and restricts the use of electronic devices while operating a vehicle.

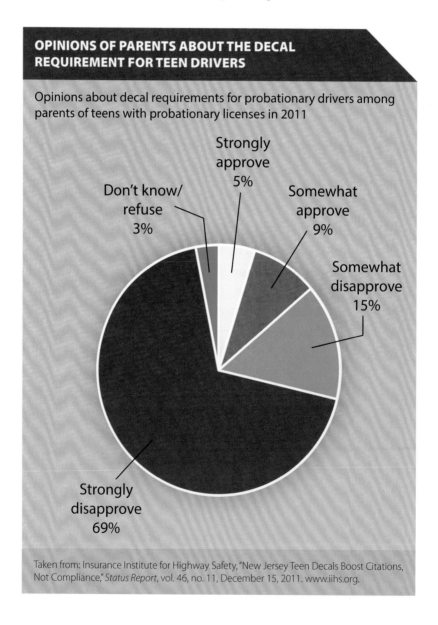

OPINIONS OF PARENTS ABOUT THE DECAL REQUIREMENT FOR TEEN DRIVERS

Opinions about decal requirements for probationary drivers among parents of teens with probationary licenses in 2011

Strongly approve
5%

Don't know/ refuse
3%

Somewhat approve
9%

Somewhat disapprove
15%

Strongly disapprove
69%

Taken from: Insurance Institute for Highway Safety, "New Jersey Teen Decals Boost Citations, Not Compliance," *Status Report*, vol. 46, no. 11, December 15, 2011. www.iihs.org.

The study used pre- and post-law statistics and trends in determining that the law prevented crashes that would have involved 1,624 teen drivers. Researchers looked at databases from Jan. 1, 2008, to May 31, 2011, in comparing monthly rates of GDL-related citations and crashes for teen drivers in the two years before Kyleigh's Law was implemented and for the year after the law took effect.

Decals Have Reduced the Crash Rate

The study found the crash rate decreased from a rate of 140.9 per 10,000 drivers before the law took effect, to 128.3 per 10,000 drivers in its aftermath. Researchers concluded that the decals increased the effectiveness of the GDL law.

In addition, researchers found that summonses for GDL violations increased 14 percent the first year after the law took effect. From May 1, 2010, to September [2011], 5,267 summonses were written.

The researchers maintain they were able to filter out other possible explanations for the reduced numbers of crashes—such as the potential effects of other laws. But that strikes us as a bit unrealistic; police, for instance, may have been more strictly enforcing the tighter restrictions of the GDL requirements that are also a part of Kyleigh's Law, independent of the decals themselves.

Police can readily spot some of the GDL violations, and gauge the youth of a driver. While the decal serves as an additional means of identification, we would hope police do not rely solely on those decals; after all, it isn't hard to simply remove the sticker to throw police off the scent. Parents have been known to encourage their children to do just that.

But there's still some encouraging news here. More research is clearly needed—and the folks at the Children's Hospital plan to do so—but these preliminary findings suggest the decals may be helping to save at least some lives, if not quite so high a number as the report's authors claim. If that's the case, and if fears of predators using the decals to identify targets are proving overblown—

and a state attorney general's study in April 2011 found only one such incident reported to police—then there is some cause for opponents to consider softening their resistance.

Besides, is that decal really *that* much different from a student or a parent putting a "Class of 2013" bumper sticker on their car?

> "*The easiest way for us to immediately cut oil consumption in this country is to raise the driving age.*"

The Minimum Driving Age Should Be Raised

William H. Longyard

In the following viewpoint William H. Longyard argues that teens should not have cars until they graduate from high school and need to get to work. In his opinion, although early-age licensing was necessary in the past, when many lived on farms and helped with work requiring vehicle use, there is no good reason for it anymore. Raising the driving age, he says, would save millions of barrels of oil a week and reduce carbon emissions, in addition to increasing teens' academic performance and involvement in school activities. But he admits that such a plan would be opposed by teens, by parents who do not want to play chauffeur, by automobile manufacturers, the insurance industry, and even mall owners. Longyard is a teacher at the Career Center in Winston-Salem, North Carolina.

Teenage Americans are much like adults: They love to talk about how concerned they are for the environment and how, as a nation, we must conserve oil, but in reality they aren't willing to make sacrifices to that end. Just go to any high-school student parking lot to see the proof.

In Europe you can't get a driver's license until you are 18, and that makes a lot of sense. Here, we allow 16-year-olds to have them, and in some states 15-year-olds, and even 14-year-olds under "hardship" conditions. Why?

Years ago, a case could be made that because so many Americans lived on farms, and their children were part of the family labor team, those children needed to drive farm equipment along public roads, or use trucks to take produce to the mill or market. But now, with a mere 2 percent of Americans involved in full-time farming, and much of that agribusiness operations that employ adult—often immigrant—workers, the case for giving children driver's licenses is weak. The easiest way for us to immediately cut oil consumption in this country is to raise the driving age to 17½.

Why 17½? Most Americans graduate from high school at 18, but some leave by 17½, and they will need to drive to jobs after they graduate. Additionally, nearly all Americans are in high school when they attain 17½, so schools can maintain their role as centers of driving instruction. Years ago, very few students drove to school during any of their four years in high school, but these days, most suburban students feel they have a God-given, inalienable right to their own wheels by the time they are 16 or 17, and no way are they going to ride the "cheese box" (school bus, think Velveeta) to school anymore, like, ya know.

School Activities Have Declined

When most students were still riding in cheese boxes—until the 1980s—school was a more significant part of their lives. With healthy memberships, athletics, drama troupes and academic clubs did a lot to keep children focused on school life, gave them positive social interaction and kept them under appropriate adult supervision when not at home. When teenage auto ownership became ubiquitous, participation in most after-school activities greatly diminished. Now school clubs are largely shell organizations that rarely meet and are established only so that administrators can list them in their required certification process and students can list them on their college applications to show how involved, energetic and capable of multitasking they are (yeah, right). The high-school glee club has gone the way of most school dances, and most high-school musicals have been cancelled for lack of participation. Kids with wheels find their own centers of entertainment, and those are usually as far away from school, and adults, as possible, sometimes at a friend's house (parents away), and sometimes in parking lots (which they tell mom is "a friend's house").

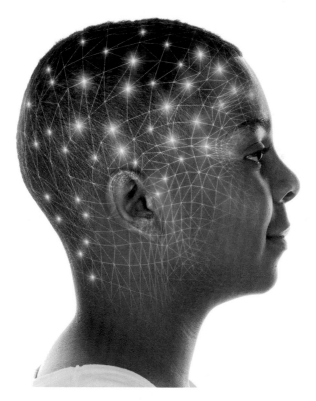

The prefrontal cortex of the human brain changes dramatically during the teenage years, causing many to doubt the judgment of teens and push for higher driving-age restrictions.
© Chad Baker/Thomas Northcu/Stone/Getty Images.

Taking 15-, 16- and half the 17-year-olds off American roads would save millions of barrels of oil a week, increase student involvement in school, increase academic achievement, decrease delinquency, save parents a fortune, cut the cost of auto insurance for everyone, require *no* student parking lots at high schools, cut carbon emissions and offer many other collateral benefits. So who would be against such a beneficial, publicly spirited plan?

Virtually everyone. Of course the kids, but also their parents, who don't want to have to go back to chauffeuring duties, and the automobile manufacturers who realize a 99 percent profit on every spoiler they tack on the back of a teenage wannabe Speed Racer's imported "tuner." Don't forget the insurance industry, which warns student drivers each year about reckless driving but reaps huge premiums from those same drivers, who pay no more attention to their agents than they do their parents. Above all, the real losers, should the driving age be raised to a sensible level, would be the mall owners, and those who pander products to teenagers with surprising large spending power, but little sense of real value.

After-School Jobs Are Unnecessary

Some will claim that students need cars to get to work, and that after-school jobs foster a sense of responsibility. However, this opens up one of the great logic howlers in all American adolescent academia:

Teacher to student: Why didn't you do your homework?

Student: I had to go to work.

Teacher: Why did you have to go to work?

Student: To pay for my car.

Teacher: Why do you need a car?

Student: To get to work.

The Teen Brain

New research shows that the human brain undergoes another period of major development between the onset of adolescence and roughly age 21.

"The biggest changes are occurring in the brain's prefrontal cortex, located right behind the forehead, which governs 'executive' thinking: our ability to use logic, make sound decisions and size up potential risks," the journal *Prevention* recently reported. The findings explain a lot about teen behavior and risk taking—particularly when driving is involved. "Knowing that this decision-making area is still under construction explains plenty about teens," the article continued. "Researchers have found that even among youths who generally show good judgment, the quality of decision-making fizzles in moments of high arousal. Emotion, whether happiness, anger or jealousy—particularly when teens are with their peers—overrides logic, making even the smart ones momentarily dumb."

Researchers now believe the phenomenon helps explain teen behavior that seems to make no sense, such as when a good student who normally respects parents' rules ends up playing a fatal game of chicken on a dark road. Teasing by peers about being afraid, for instance, can temporarily short-circuit a teen's otherwise hardwired knowledge about what's wisely safe or stupidly dangerous.

William Triplett, "Teen Driving: Should States Impose Tougher Restrictions?," CQ Researcher, vol. 15, no. 1, January 7, 2005.

Is an after-school job, at the expense of academic performance, a worthwhile trade off? Isn't the car-culture a root cause of our educational crisis?

If we are to begin to get a hold on the over-use of oil in this country, the fastest way to do so is to cut out young driving. Yes, when someone graduates from high school and enters the job market, he or she must have access to an automobile, but for the vast majority of Americans that is not until 17½. Let that be the age for a license in this country. Will it happen? Not as long as parents can't say no to children who have tantrums when asked to ride a cheese box, and politicians can't take on the vested interests of car makers, insurance companies and retailers. But we all want to do something to save the environment, don't we?

> *"Instead of simply raising the driving age, we should . . . treat [teen driving] as an experience issue, not an age issue."*

The Minimum Driving Age Should Not Be Raised

Mike Rogers

In the following viewpoint Mike Rogers points out that since young people do not get the diseases older people do, it is only natural that accidents, and auto accidents in particular, are the leading cause of death among them. He argues that experience, not age, is the main factor in safe driving, and that if the minimum driving age were raised, so would be the age of the drivers with the deadliest accidents. Rogers is a truck driver, and he has seen that the most dangerous truck drivers are those with less than two years of experience, even though they usually do not get commercial driver's licenses before they are twenty-one years old. Furthermore, he believes that teens should learn to be independent and that parents are the best judge of when their kids are mature enough to drive.

The legal driving age has been a constant debate and every few years another log is thrown onto the fire. Should we really raise the legal age to drive? Would it save lives? If so, how high

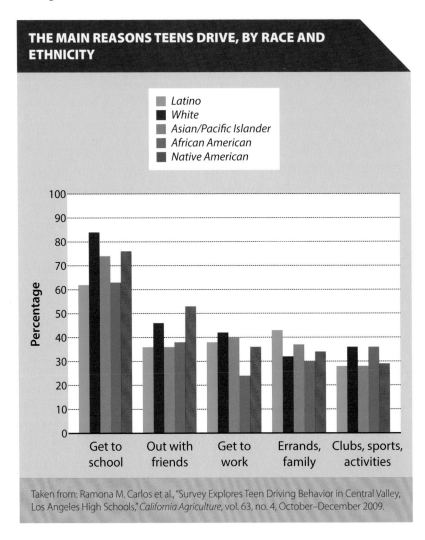

THE MAIN REASONS TEENS DRIVE, BY RACE AND ETHNICITY

Latino
White
Asian/Pacific Islander
African American
Native American

Taken from: Ramona M. Carlos et al., "Survey Explores Teen Driving Behavior in Central Valley, Los Angeles High Schools," *California Agriculture*, vol. 63, no. 4, October–December 2009.

should we raise it? Currently, most states allow for teen drivers to apply for a drivers permit 6 months after their 15th birthday. Some say this is way too soon.

It's an unfortunate truth, but auto accidents are the leading cause of death among teenagers. A 16-year-old is almost twice as likely to die in a car crash than a 30-year-old. And with new issues such as cell phone driving, texting while driving, and other forms of distracted driving, there is good reason to debate this issue. If we can take the most dangerous drivers off the road, we will not only save the lives of young adults, but we will also make the roadways safer for everyone else.

Driving Is Deadly for All Age Groups

What's interesting is the leading cause of death for 15- to 24-year olds is auto accidents. They are the only age group where this is true. However, car crashes are the leading cause of accidental death in all age groups over 4 years old! Let's face it, 15- to 24-year olds aren't plagued with disease and sickness like older folks are. So it's only natural that their leading cause of death will be accidental, and will also be the leading accidental death for nearly every age group. So the stats aren't exactly cut and dry.

Is age really the biggest factor to consider? If we raise the legal driving age to, say, 17 years old, wouldn't 17-year-olds have the highest accident rate simply due to lack of experience? Many argue that our decision making skills aren't fully developed at 16 (the legal age at which a license can actually be obtained). However, this is mostly unsubstantiated evidence and since every person develops differently, a blanketed law is going to punish those who are ready.

I'm a truck driver and see this with new truckers. The legal age to receive a commercial drivers license is 18 years old, but most don't obtain their commercial drivers license until after the age of 21. The most dangerous truck drivers on the road are those with under 2 years of experience, regardless of age. It's likely that if we simply raise the driving age, we will only shift the "problem drivers" to a higher age bracket. . . .

Major Issues with Raising the Legal Driving Age

Aside from young teens hating the idea, do we really want our kids dependent upon us for everything? Do we really want to chauffeur our kids everywhere, up until the point they graduate high school, go off to college, or even join the military? Getting

The chance of a sixteen-year-old being involved in an accident is twice that of a thirty-year-old, especially with the advent of the cell phone and the ubiquity of texting and driving. © Yellow Dog Productions/The Image Bank/Getty Images.

a drivers license is a "right of passage" so to speak. We have to "let go" at some point or another. Most teens don't have access to public transit. We need to let them have some freedom. We need to let them get jobs. We need to let them grow up. And learning to drive is one of the very first steps into adulthood. The world is a dangerous place, but we must "let go" at some point.

Every child and every teenager develops in their own unique way. Instead of forcing the government to make blanketed laws, let's leave things the way they are and force parents to be parents. Allow mom and dad to decide if their child should drive or not. Who knows a teenager better than the teenager's guardian?

Most states have developed a "graduated licensing" program, which has proven to be successful. This includes more time behind the wheel with a supervised and licensed adult, more classroom time, and zero tolerance policies for traffic violations (a violation could result in further training or even license revocation).

Limiting forms of distracted driving is also a good idea. Some states have a graduated rider program. At first, no passengers are allowed unless it's an adult. After some experience, they can bring more passengers on board. Zero tolerance cell phone use and driving curfew laws have also proven to be successful.

Traditionally, we have given full license privileges to 16-year-olds. Instead of simply raising the driving age, we should continue to implement programs which slowly give more driving privileges to teens as they prove themselves to be safe, trustworthy drivers. Let's treat this as an experience issue, not an age issue.

> *"The use of electronic devices is the leader among [teen] distracted driving behaviors."*

Electronics Top Distractions for Teen Drivers

David Morgan

In the following viewpoint David Morgan reports on a study of teen driving behavior made by the American Automobile Association's Foundation for Traffic Safety. In the study, video recordings were made inside the cars of the fifty families who participated. Recording was triggered by events such as sudden braking or an abrupt turn, and it was found that in nearly half of such cases, the driver had looked away from the road for a few seconds preceding the event. The most common cause of distraction was texting or talking on the phone, which girls did more than boys. Other frequent causes were loud conversations and horseplay in the car. Morgan is a reporter for CBS News.

A new study of teen driving behavior has found that the use of electronic devices is the leader among distracted driving behaviors, and that teenage girls are twice as likely as boys to use cell phones or other electronic devices while driving.

The findings, from a study of video taken of young drivers, were released Monday by the AAA Foundation for Traffic Safety.

Talking on the phone or texting while driving was the most common behavior that distracted young drivers, more so than adjusting controls, grooming, eating or drinking, or engaging in horseplay or loud conversations with passengers.

The findings are notable given that distracted driving behaviors are believed to contribute to traffic accidents, injuries and fatalities—and traffic crashes remain the leading cause of death for young Americans.

"This new study provides the best view we've had about how and when teens engage in distracted driving behaviors believed to contribute to making car crashes the leading cause of death for teenagers," said AAA Foundation President and CEO Peter Kissinger.

The study used data derived from video recordings taken inside the cars of 50 families with young drivers participating in the study, to capture drivers' behavior. Data recording was triggered by certain events—sudden braking, an abrupt turn—during unsupervised driving times. Data by older, more experienced sibling drivers was also captured, resulting in 24,085 driving clips of 52 teens taken over a six-month period.

More than 7,500 clips were selected for analysis, with sample sizes factoring in different driving patterns, distracting passengers, etc.

Sixty-three percent of drivers were age 16, 17 percent 17, and 19 percent were 18. More than two-thirds—69 percent—were female. The vehicles being driven were passenger cars (56 percent), SUVs (17 percent), minivans (15 percent) and pickup trucks (12 percent).

Driver Behavior

In 6.7 percent of all driving clips, teenage drivers were observed using an electronic device—two-thirds of whom were observed holding a cell phone to their ear. Female drivers were twice as

Although using electronic devices while driving is the most common distraction, eating while driving is also shown to cause unsafe driving practices. © Spencer Rowell/The Image Bank/ Getty Images.

likely as males to be observed using an electronic device. Nine drivers (17 percent) did not use any electronic device.

The study noted that use of electronic devices was actually twice as high among the 14 slightly older, more experienced high school-age siblings than among the younger members of the test group. All but one of the older drivers were observed using an electronic device at least once. Of the younger drivers, eight of the 38 target teens did not use any electronic device at all.

The tendency among new drivers to adhere to prohibitions against using cell phones or texting while driving may fade after time, the study suggests. The authors call out police in North

Carolina (where the video data recordings were made), writing, "There has been no concerted effort to enforce the teen driver cell phone restriction in North Carolina, which teens may realize after several months of driving." [According to court records, fewer than 50 citations were issued for violations of teen driver cell phone restriction during 2010.]

Other distracted driver behaviors included: adjusting controls; eating or drinking; personal hygiene; reading; turning around; reaching for an object; and communicating with a person outside the vehicle.

Eyes off the Road

In nearly half (45 percent) of the abrupt driving events which triggered the data recording, the driver looked away from the roadway at some point within the 10 seconds preceding the event. Most did only briefly—two seconds or less—but 12 percent looked away for at least four seconds. Also, females looked away more often than males.

The reason for looking away? Drivers were three times as likely to be looking at an electronic device than anything else.

Distractions Involving Passengers

When passengers were present, loud conversations were recorded in 12.2 percent of the distracted driving clips. Horseplay was observed in 6.3 percent of clips.

Males were found to be twice as likely to turn around while driving, and more likely to communicate with people outside the vehicle.

Perhaps not surprisingly, parents or other adults present in the car corresponded with a significant reduction in distracting behaviors.

Potentially Serious Events

Also studied was how the distracted driving related to potentially serious events, including near-collisions or high G-force

TEENS AND DISTRACTED DRIVING

Have you ever experienced or done any of the following?

	All Teens 12–17	Older Teens 16–17	Cell Users 16–17	Texters 16–17
Been in a car when the driver was texting	48%	64%	70%	73%
Been in a car when the driver used a cell phone in a way that put themselves or others in danger	40%	48%	51%	52%
Talked on a cell phone while driving	n/a	43%	52%	54%
Texted while driving	n/a	26%	32%	34%

Data from Pew Internet and American Life Project, Teens and Mobile Phones Survey conducted from June 26 to September 24, 2009.

Taken from: Mary Madden and Amanda Lenhart, "Teens and Distracted Driving," Pew Research Internet Project, November 16, 2009.

events. Just over half (52 percent) of the clips analyzed involved such serious events. While sample size precluded finding causal relationships between electronic devices or horseplay with serious events, loud conversations were six times more likely to be involved, and horseplay was a consistent factor.

Driving Conditions

There did not seem to be a relationship between the frequency of driving distractions and traffic or roadway conditions, with only a slightly lower tendency during rain conditions.

The study, Distracted Driving Among Newly Licensed Teen Drivers, was prepared by researchers at the University of North Carolina Highway Safety Research Center, and is the first study to use in-car video recordings to study teen distracted driving.

> *"My life has changed forever because I was a distracted driver. . . . I killed my best friend and caused injury to . . . my grandparents."*

A Teen Tells How He Killed His Best Friend Through Distracted Driving

Personal Narrative

Matthew Verrinder

In the following viewpoint Matthew Verrinder tells of the tragedy he brought about through distracted driving. He got into a road race with another friend, driving on the wrong side of the road, and because he was so intent on winning, he did not notice the speed limit sign or the stop sign at an intersection. He crashed into another car, which flew across the road into a wooded area. His best friend, who was beside him in his car, was killed. The car that Verrinder hit was carrying an older couple, who were seriously injured and nearly died. Only later did Verrinder find out that they were his own grandparents. Verrinder won a Carter Mario Arrive Alive scholarship for this essay. At the time of its publication he was attending the University of New Haven in Connecticut.

It was the evening of a beautiful spring day in April of 2005 that my life was forever changed. I had spent a fun afternoon with a bunch of friends. The weather was so nice that day. We were all in the mood for ice cream.

We all decided to go to McDonald's. There were six of us, so we decided to take two cars. Before getting into the cars, my friend challenged me to a race to the end of North Coe Lane in Ansonia [Connecticut]. It was a side street that was straight, flat and probably a half mile long. My friends always made fun of my car. I wanted to show them that I had a car with "balls" and finally shut them up. It did not take me more than a few seconds to make a decision that forever changed my life.

As the race began, I was in the left lane of the road and my friend was in the right lane. I was so distracted because I wanted to win the race. All of my common sense and safe driving was gone . . . in a flash . . . because of a challenge . . . to win a road race. I drove down the wrong side of the road. I did not see the black and white speed limit sign that said "SPEED LIMIT 25." I did not obey the speed limit sign.

I was so focused on staying ahead of my friend and winning the race. I did not apply my brakes in time to stop at the stop sign. By the time I realized that I needed to stop at the intersection, it was too late to make my car stop. I left a trail of skid marks about fifty feet long.

I blew the stop sign and hit another car coming up Pulaski Highway. That car went flying across the opposite lane into the wooded area of a private property. The noise from the screeching tires and the twisting of metal is something I will never forget.

My car stopped dead in the middle of the intersection and my heart nearly stopped when I realized my best friend was no longer in the front seat with me. Where was he? Was this a joke? He had his seat belt on didn't he? I was in shock. When I finally came to my senses, I realized that he had been ejected from the car. He died immediately as his body hit the ground.

Driving

There were two passengers in the car that I hit. They were an older couple. As they sat in their crushed car, they held hands together and prayed as the firemen cut them out of the car with the Jaws of Life. They thought they were both going to die that night. Their injuries were very serious and required several surgeries

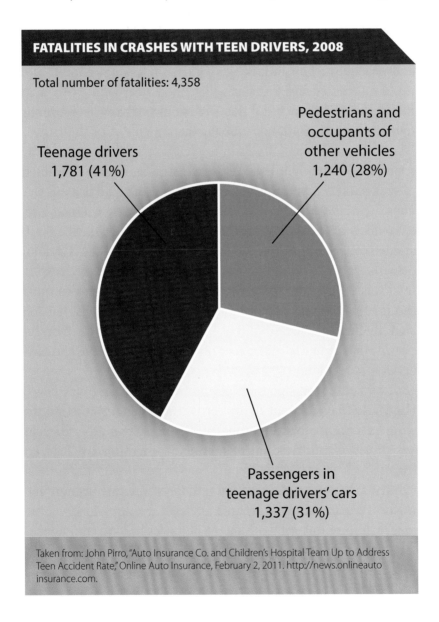

FATALITIES IN CRASHES WITH TEEN DRIVERS, 2008

Total number of fatalities: 4,358

Teenage drivers
1,781 (41%)

Pedestrians and occupants of other vehicles
1,240 (28%)

Passengers in teenage drivers' cars
1,337 (31%)

Taken from: John Pirro, "Auto Insurance Co. and Children's Hospital Team Up to Address Teen Accident Rate," Online Auto Insurance, February 2, 2011. http://news.onlineauto insurance.com.

and therapy. Their lives have changed forever because of their injuries.

My life has changed forever because I was a distracted driver. I did serve some jail time for my actions. But jail time is nothing compared to the fact that I killed my best friend and caused injury to other people and they have not been able to fully recover from their injuries.

I am here today to say that what happened to me, *can happen to you*. It is a privilege to drive, a right that you earn. Your car can become a weapon in a moment of poor judgment.

Listen to your parents' words of wisdom. Use your head and be safe. Don't drive distracted. Don't use your cell phone or text. Don't participate in races or road rage. Wear your seat belt. Obey the speed limit.

By the way, I forgot to tell you one important detail. The older couple in the other car . . . they are my grandparents.

> "The [teen] court . . . [is] trying to nip
> poor driving habits and behavior in
> the bud."

Teen-Run Traffic Courts Can Help Improve Teens' Poor Driving Habits

Sara Jean Green

In the following viewpoint Sara Jean Green describes the youth traffic court that is being established in Seattle, Washington, similar to the many successful youth courts elsewhere in the nation. The court will be staffed by high school students who, with training by university law students, will serve as judges, attorneys, and jurors. Teens who go before the court must be under eighteen, have pled guilty to their traffic law violation, and have not been involved in an accident involving injury. The court will be based on the philosophy of restorative justice, imposing not fines but rather sentences such as writing apology letters or performing community service. The legal experts in charge believe that teens are more affected by a judgment from their peers than by lectures from adults. Green is a reporter for the Seattle Times.

Seattle Municipal Court Judge Karen Donohue knows there's nothing scarier for parents than handing over a set of car keys to a teenage driver.

She also knows that when adults talk—be it a parent, a teacher, or even a judge—what teens tend to hear is a lot of "white noise." And when young people make a mistake behind the wheel, it's often their parents who end up paying tickets and dealing with increased car-insurance rates.

Changing that dynamic is behind the launch of the city's first youth traffic court, which will begin hearing cases later this month involving Seattle drivers younger than 18. The court will be staffed by 22 Garfield High School students. The Garfield students will get community service credit and have been trained by law students from Seattle University to act as judges, prosecutors, defense attorneys, bailiffs, court clerks and jurors. Garfield was chosen because of its proximity to Seattle University.

But instead of handing out fines, the court will tailor sanctions based on the philosophy of restorative justice, according to Margaret Fisher, co-director of the Seattle youth traffic court along with Donohue and Seattle Municipal Court Magistrate Lisa Leone. A teen may be ordered to write an essay for the school paper, or perhaps do yard work for someone whose vehicle was damaged. Teens who go before the youth court will also be required to serve on two future juries.

If they successfully complete their sentences, the teen defendants will see their tickets dismissed and keep their driving records clean—which will mean no insurance-rate increases for Mom and Dad.

The average fine for a moving violation is $124, while driving without proof of insurance—a common youth violation—carries a $550 fine. A standard speeding ticket costs $154, and speeding in a school zone, $189.

"In my experience, I've seen kids for running stop signs and running traffic lights. But I think the No. 1 [offense] is speeding and speeding through school zones," said Donohue.

Restorative Justice

Restorative justice outlines an alternative philosophy for addressing crime. When viewed from a restorative lens, crime is a violation of people and relationships—the relationships between the offender and his or her family, friends, victims, and the community—as opposed to merely an act against the state. In essence, restorative justice focuses on repairing harm and rebuilding relationships through a process that involves stakeholders in an active and respectful way, while emphasizing the community's role in problem solving. From a practical perspective, it requires the juvenile justice system to respond to crime by devoting attention to

- Enabling offenders to understand the harm caused by their behavior and to make amends to their victims and communities.
- Building on offenders' strengths and increasing offenders' competencies.
- Giving victims an opportunity to participate in justice processes.
- Protecting the public through a process in which the individual victims, the community, and offenders are all active stakeholders.

Tracy M. Godwin, "The Role of Restorative Justice in Teen Courts: A Preliminary Look," National Youth Court Center, 2001. www.youthcourt.net.

"Having had teen drivers in my family and seeing kids who come through court, I think this is a great opportunity" for teens to truly understand the impact their bad driving can have on the community, she said.

Garfield High freshman Clare Fuget, who turns 16 in September [2012], acknowledged that she and her peers rarely think of consequences until after the fact. "We're kind of heat-of-the-moment, that-looks-like-fun" people, she said. While young people may be impulsive and reckless at times, she said it's important their voices are heard and perspectives taken into account. "A lot of times adults make our decisions or parents make our decisions, and we're not OK with that. We need to speak for ourselves," she said. ". . . We can relate to each other more."

On Monday, Fuget will play the role of prosecutor in a scripted hearing before city officials, legal professionals and police representatives. While the program's kickoff will be a dry run based on a fictional scenario, Fuget and her fellow youth-court participants will begin hearing real cases March 26. After that, the court will convene once a month and hear up to five cases per session.

"Basically, we're trying to nip poor driving habits and behavior in the bud," said Forrest Smith, one of six Seattle University law students who are mentoring the youth-court participants.

Teenagers in Colorado participate in Teen Court, where juveniles are tried by a jury of other minors, only the judge is an adult, and the verdict is binding. © Hyoung Chang/Denver Post via Getty Images.

To qualify, drivers must be under 18 and have been ticketed in Seattle. They must admit to committing the traffic infractions for which they were stopped and agree to have their cases heard by the youth courts. Teens involved in injury accidents or under investigation for more serious crimes such as vehicular homicide are not eligible, nor are young drivers who have previously gone before the youth court.

Fisher wrote the American Bar Association's curriculum for youth courts in 2000 and has authored reports on youth courts for the U.S. Department of Justice. A distinguished practitioner in residence at Seattle University's law school, Fisher is convinced youth courts "are the best way for young people to learn about fairness and justice."

"It's a very maturing process," Fisher said of teens who have their cases adjudicated by a group of peers.

There are more than 1,000 youth courts (including five or six in Washington) across the country, up from 78 in 1994, according to the National Association of Youth Courts. Some youth courts handle criminal diversions, while others focus on teen truancy, said Fisher.

"Kids are so inventive and creative" in handing down sentences, Fisher said.

Ordering a teen to write an apology letter, perform community service, or even go on a ride-along with police can have a bigger impact on a young person's driving habits "than watching all the gory movies in the world," she said, referring to the kinds of films typically shown in driver's ed classes.

> *"Aside from the harsh criminal and civil penalties given for an underage DUI, there are grave social consequences for a minor convicted of a DUI."*

Teens Arrested for Drinking and Driving Face Harsher Consequences than Do Adult Offenders

Freeadvice.com

In the following viewpoint an attorney explains the consequences a teen incurs if caught drinking and driving. Teens are arrested for driving under the influence (DUI) if their blood alcohol level is above zero (or in some states, 0.02)—not 0.08 as is the case for adults; teens do not have to be intoxicated to be so charged. The teen's driver's license is immediately suspended or revoked and the car may be impounded. Penalties imposed by courts are harsh; there may be a jail sentence for a first offense, and there always will be for a repeat offense. Moreover, a record of a teen DUI conviction must be disclosed on college and employment applications, which may prevent a student from pursuing his or her chosen career. FreeAdvice.com is an informational website staffed by attorneys and other legal professionals.

More than 3000 teenagers die every year in drunk driving accidents. Further, the rate of alcohol-related automobile accidents is higher for drivers between the ages of 16–20 than it is for adults over the age of 21. The rate is higher for teenagers because teenagers are generally inexperienced with alcohol, they take greater risks, and they exercise less caution. Teenagers put themselves and others in a grave amount of danger when they get behind the wheel of a car while under the influence. It is for these reasons that the laws and penalties for teenage drunk driving are tough throughout the country.

Zero-tolerance laws were introduced in the early 1980s in reaction to the high level of teenage drunk driving injuries and deaths across the country. Because of the seriousness of teen drunk driving and in response to federal financial incentives, all states have now implemented zero-tolerance laws. Zero-tolerance laws have two components. The first component is *Illegal per se* laws; *per se* means in and of itself. This means that if

Many studies show that the rate of alcohol-related car accidents is far higher among drivers ages sixteen to twenty than it is for adults twenty-one or older. © Stock Connection Distribution/ Alamy.

a minor under 21 years of age is caught driving with a negligible percentage of alcohol in his or her blood, they will be arrested for DUI [driving under the influence] immediately.

Some states will charge a minor with a DUI if the blood alcohol limit is over 0.00 percent. Most states set their zero-tolerance laws at 0.02. This is different from the laws for adults where a 0.08 level of alcohol is required for a DUI. The second component of the zero-tolerance laws is the *administrative per se* laws. This means that if the minor is caught driving with any level of alcohol in the system, their license will be automatically suspended or revoked by the Department of Motor Vehicles (DMV) or the Registry of Motor Vehicles (RMV).

These penalties are in addition to whatever penalties the court imposes. Zero-tolerance laws have been subject to criticism by people who believe that the laws unfairly punish minors who may be bringing home an intoxicated friend. However, zero-tolerance laws have proven to be an effective sanction for minors, and since they have been implemented, the rate of teenage deaths and injuries in automobile accidents has gone down. Having a license is, after all, the ultimate statement of independence for many teens.

Consequences of Teenage DUI Convictions

Punishments for teenagers that are found guilty of a DUI vary by state, but are generally harsher for first time offenders than are punishments given to adult first time offenders. This is because minors face penalties for both underage drinking and for driving under the influence. If the minor's blood alcohol content (BAC) is anywhere from 0.05–0.07 percent and above, they can be charged with underage DUI and an adult DUI, which can increase the penalties further.

Often other charges will accompany the DUI offense, such as violation of Child Endangerment Laws, minor in possession of alcohol, possession of an altered or fictitious ID card, soliciting

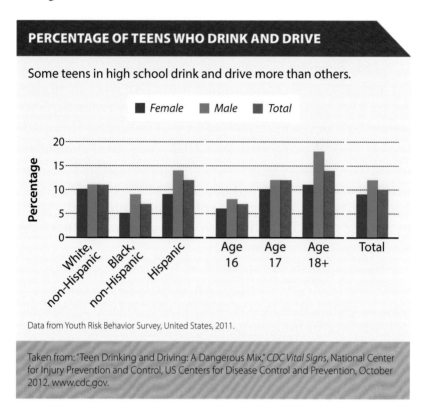

PERCENTAGE OF TEENS WHO DRINK AND DRIVE

Some teens in high school drink and drive more than others.

■ *Female* ■ *Male* ■ *Total*

Data from Youth Risk Behavior Survey, United States, 2011.

Taken from: "Teen Drinking and Driving: A Dangerous Mix," *CDC Vital Signs*, National Center for Injury Prevention and Control, US Centers for Disease Control and Prevention, October 2012. www.cdc.gov.

alcohol from an adult, and distributing alcohol to other minors. In most states, the minor's DUI will be charged as a class one misdemeanor, which will remain on their record as an adult. The court may also impose community service as a punishment and up to thousands of dollars in fines. The teen's license may also be suspended for up to two years and many states will require the minor to submit proof of financial responsibility before their license is reinstated.

In some states, a teen DUI conviction can result in up to one year in jail for a first offense. Minors that have been caught drunk driving more than once, as well as minors who are involved in drunk driving accidents, will always receive a jail sentence. Sentences range from a few days to several years, depending on the severity of the case.

A teen DUI conviction can also result in probation for a period of 3–5 years. The minor may also be ordered to undergo a diversion program, such as Mothers Against Drunk Driving (MADD) or other drug and alcohol education classes. If the minor's BAC is especially high, he or she may have to complete an inpatient alcohol treatment program.

After the teen or minor has his license reinstated, he or she may still have to drive under the watchful eye of the courts. In these cases, the court may order the minor to install an ignition interlock device on his or her car or on the car that the minor drives the most frequently. This will have to be done at the minor's own expense.

In some cases, the court may choose to impound the car, instead of requiring an ignition interlock device. Further, hardship or conditional licenses are not as widely available for minors convicted of DUIs. A hardship or conditional license is granted in cases where the convicted must drive his car in order to commute to work and school. These types of licenses allow the convicted minor to drive to locations approved by the courts, and nowhere else.

Consequences for Refusing Alcohol Testing in Suspected DUI Stops

Minors that refuse to submit to alcohol testing may lose their license for up to three years in some states. This is because most state laws use the implied consent principle, which says that once you are given a license to drive on public roads and highways, you implicitly give your consent to be tested for sobriety. Refusal to submit to testing is often seen as an admission of guilt. Further, this may not prevent a DUI charge, since the police can use other evidence to show that the teenager was under the influence, such as erratic driving or the smell of alcohol in the minor's breath.

What this means is, if the minor refuses to submit to testing and is convicted of a DUI, he or she will receive a consecutive license suspension for both offenses. In most states, minors that refuse to submit to testing face the same legal and social consequences as an underage DUI.

Aside from the harsh criminal and civil penalties given for an underage DUI, there are grave social consequences for a minor convicted of a DUI. A minor who is convicted of DUI must disclose this information on all college applications. This may not prevent the minor from getting into college, but it will certainly be a strike against them. Failure to list the DUI on the application can result in automatic dismissal if the college later learns of the DUI.

In many states, students that are convicted of DUIs cannot continue their majors in education or pre-law. Further, starting a career with a DUI conviction may be difficult for the minor. Many jobs ask applicants to list any prior convictions. Since most states classify a DUI conviction as a Class 1 misdemeanor, the minor's record will be blemished well into adulthood.

While a prior conviction will not be an absolute bar to employment, it may sometimes sway an employer's decision to hire them. A civil judgment against a minor can also last years, meaning that their future wages can be garnished. The teenager may also face social stigma as well and incarceration could mean a loss of employment and educational possibilities.

While the punishments for underage drinking and teenage drunk driving are tough, it is important to know that the minor still has the same rights in the legal system as adults. This means that the prosecutor must show all the elements of the charges, including that the minor was driving and that the stop was for a legitimate reason. Because of the penalties and life consequences that a DUI will have for a minor, it usually makes sense to try and fight the DUI in court.

"We conclude that suspending . . . driving privileges for underage consumption of alcohol . . . does not violate defendants' constitutional rights."

Losing Driving Privileges for Underage Drinking Is Constitutional

The Illinois Supreme Court Opinion

Thomas L. Kilbride

In the following viewpoint the Supreme Court of Illinois rules that a state law may provide that teens lose their driver's licenses for underage drinking even when not in a car. The defendants argued that this law is unconstitutional on the basis of a previous case that held unconstitutional another law providing for the loss of driver's licenses for an offense not involving a car. But, the court decided, the two cases were different because in the prior one, the offense bore no relationship to driving, whereas in the opinion of the judges it is reasonable to assume that a teen who disobeys the law by drinking may also disobey it by driving afterward. It ruled that the loss of a driver's license was intended not as punishment,

Thomas L. Kilbride, Court's opinion, *People v. Boeckmann*, Supreme Court of Illinois, June 24, 2010.

but as a means of protecting the public. Thomas L. Kilbride was serving a three-year term as the Chief Justice of the Supreme Court of Illinois at the time of this writing.

The defendants in this consolidated appeal, Zachary R. Boeckmann and Chelsey M. Maschhoff, were each charged with unlawful consumption of alcohol by a person under 21 years of age. The defendants filed motions to declare unconstitutional sections 6-206(a)(38) and (a)(43) of the Vehicle Code. Those sections generally authorize the Secretary of State to suspend or revoke a defendant's driving privileges upon conviction or disposition of court supervision for the charged offenses.

Defendants alleged sections 6-206(a)(38) and (a)(43) violated their constitutional rights to due process and equal protection of the law. Defendants pled guilty to unlawful consumption of alcohol as charged. The trial court placed them on court supervision for 90 days and, the following day, declared sections 6-206(a)(38) and (a)(43) unconstitutional. . . .

The trial court held this court's decision in *People v. Lindner,* (1989), controlled because a vehicle was not involved in the commission of the offenses. The defendants' other constitutional challenges based on the equal protection and proportionate penalties clauses were rejected by the trial court. . . .

The Court's Analysis

The [Illinois] Secretary [of State] contends the trial court erred in finding section 6-206(a)(43) violates due process as applied to the defendants. According to the Secretary, suspension of the defendants' driving privileges for unlawful consumption of alcohol bears a rational relationship to the legitimate governmental interest in highway safety. The Secretary maintains that preventing young people who consume alcohol from driving is a reasonable means of furthering the interest in highway safety. The Secretary also argues the suspension of defendants' driving privileges under section 6-206(a)(43) is a reasonable means of promoting the legitimate public interest in deterring underage consumption of alcohol.

Citing this court's decision in *Lindner*, defendants contend that suspending their driving privileges does not bear a rational relationship to the public interest in the safe operation of motor vehicles because no vehicle was involved in the commission of their offenses. Defendants further argue suspension of driving privileges in all cases of underage consumption of alcohol is not a reasonable means of promoting the public interest in highway safety. . . .

This court has held a driver's license is a nonfundamental property interest. When a statute does not impact a fundamental constitutional right, the applicable standard for reviewing whether it conforms with substantive due process is the rational basis test. Generally, a statute violates the constitutional guarantee of due process under the rational basis test if it does not bear a rational relationship to a legitimate legislative purpose, or is arbitrary or discriminatory. In applying the rational basis test, we must identify the public interest the statute is intended to protect, determine whether the statute bears a rational relationship to that interest, and examine whether the method chosen to protect or further that interest is reasonable.

Rational basis review is highly deferential, but it is not "toothless." Legislation must be upheld if there is a conceivable basis for finding it is rationally related to a legitimate state interest. The legislature's judgments in drafting a statute are not subject to judicial fact finding and "may be based on rational speculation unsupported by evidence or empirical data." *Arangold v. Zehnder*.

The Intent of the Law

We must first determine the public interest section 6-206(a)(43) is intended to protect. In examining the public interest of similar Vehicle Code provisions in *Lindner*, this court considered the Vehicle Code as a whole, the substantive provisions of the challenged sections, and the Vehicle Code's statement of purpose.

We observed that the stated purpose of the Vehicle Code contained in section 6-204(a) is preventing people from driving if they demonstrate an unfitness to operate a motor vehicle safely. Further, the challenged statute sections generally enumerate offenses connected to operating or owning a vehicle safely and legally. We concluded, therefore, that the challenged provisions were intended to protect the public interest in "the safe and legal operation and ownership of motor vehicles."

The statement of purpose, in section 6-204 is still directed at preventing people from driving after they have shown an unfitness to operate a vehicle safely.

Additionally, the statute section challenged here describes offenses and behavior largely connected to operating a motor vehicle safely and legally. Accordingly, as in *Lindner*, we conclude section 6-206 is intended to promote the safe and legal operation and ownership of motor vehicles.

We must, therefore, determine whether section 6-206(a)(43) bears a reasonable relationship to the public interest in the safe and legal operation and ownership of motor vehicles. As applied in this case, section 6-206(a)(43) provides for suspension of driving privileges when a person has received court supervision for underage consumption of alcohol. The statute will be upheld if a conceivable basis exists for finding it rationally related to the identified legitimate public interest.

Here, the General Assembly may have believed that a young person who has a driver's license and consumes alcohol illegally may take the additional step of driving after consuming alcohol. It is reasonable to believe a young person disobeying the law against underage consumption of alcohol may also lack the judgment to decline to drive after drinking. Preventing young people from driving after consuming alcohol unquestionably furthers the public interest in the safe and legal operation of motor vehicles.

Defendants, nonetheless, contend this court's decision in *Lindner* compels a finding that section 6-206(a)(43) violates due process. According to defendants, *Lindner* held that suspending driving privileges violates the constitutional guarantee of due process if a vehicle was not involved in the commission of the offense.

In *Lindner*, the dispute focused on identifying the public interest the challenged statute was intended to protect. This court noted that the State apparently conceded the unconstitutionality of the statute if the defendant's argument on the statute's purpose

A Divided Court in the *People v. Boeckmann* Decision

The decision in [*People v.*] *Boeckmann* divided the court into writing lead, concurring, and dissenting opinions with two justices behind each faction. This split shows the complexity of the issue and how the justices can agree on so much, but in the end come to different conclusions. The lead opinion chose not to overrule [*People v.*] *Lindner* in finding the statute constitutional, but rather contorted the precedent to what the remaining four justices considered "meaningless." The concurring opinion then goes on to find the same conclusion as the lead, but does so by overruling *Lindner* without either party even arguing good cause to do so. Finally, the dissent agrees with the trial court and the concurring justices that by following the precedent laid out in *Lindner*, this statute must be found unconstitutional. The dissenters, however, agree with the lead opinion that *stare decisis* prohibits the court from overruling *Lindner* without cause. If a case similar to *Boeckmann* were to be brought up on appeal in the future, a reversal would not be implausible as so little separated the opinions of the justices who found the law constitutional from those who found it unconstitutional.

Colby Hathaway, "Drivers License Suspension for Offenses Not Involving a Motor Vehicle in Illinois," Northern Illinois University Law Review, vol. 32, 2012, p. 378.

were accepted. We agreed with the defendant's argument that the statute served the public interest in the safe and legal operation and ownership of motor vehicles. Without any argument from the State on the point, we then concluded revocation of the defendant's driver's license did not bear a reasonable relationship to that public interest because a vehicle was not involved in the commission of the defendant's sex offenses.

Defendants assert this court should follow "[t]he principle in *Lindner* that if no car is involved, like here, then to suspend driving privileges would violate due process." Defendants, however, rely on a narrow reading of *Lindner*. We have subsequently explained the rationale in *Lindner*, stating "[t]here was no rational relationship between sex offenders and safe driving, and on that basis the statute was found unconstitutional." *People v. Adams.* We have further explained that in *Lindner*, the revocation of the defendant's driver's license did not bear a rational relationship to the public interest to be served because the defendant's crimes "neither involved a motor vehicle nor bore any rational relationship to his ability to drive a motor vehicle safely." [*People v.*] *Jones, Lindner.* Accordingly, the rationale in *Lindner* is broader than simply determining whether a vehicle was involved in the offense. Rather, the critical determination is whether the revocation of driving privileges bears a rational relationship to the public interest in the safe operation of motor vehicles.

The Law Supports a Rational Public Interest

In *Lindner*, there was no connection between the defendant's sex offenses and his ability to drive a motor vehicle safely. In contrast, defendants' underage consumption of alcohol would certainly impact their ability to drive a motor vehicle safely. The legislature could have rationally believed young people who have a driver's license and consume alcohol illegally may also drive after consuming alcohol, regardless of whether a motor vehicle is involved in the charged offense. On this point, we note that the appellate court has held suspension of driving privileges for the use of false identification in an attempt to obtain alcohol is rationally related to the safe and legal operation of a motor vehicle. The appellate court held the legislature could rationally speculate that licensees under 21 years of age may use false identification to obtain alcohol, leading on balance to an increase in driving under the influence or driving after consuming alcohol. We likewise conclude that suspension of defendants' driving privileges for underage consumption of alcohol bears a rational relationship to the safe and legal operation of motor vehicles.

Defendants also contend that suspending their driving privileges is not a reasonable method of protecting the public interest because they had no plans to drive after consuming alcohol. As we have found, there is a rational relationship between suspending a person's driver's license for underage consumption of alcohol and the safe and legal operation of motor vehicles, regardless of whether a motor vehicle is involved in the particular offense. The legislature may reasonably determine a young person consuming alcohol under the legal age may also drive after drinking. Preventing young people from driving after consuming alcohol furthers the public interest in the safe and legal operation of motor vehicles. We, therefore, conclude that suspension of defendants' driving privileges for underage consumption of alcohol is a reasonable method of promoting the public interest despite the absence of a motor vehicle or plans to drive in these circumstances. . . .

The special concurrence [an opinion written by a judge who agreed with the decision but not with the reasons for it] asserts *Lindner* was wrongly decided and should be overruled because it defined the public purpose of the statute too narrowly. The parties do not ask this court to overrule *Lindner* or present any argument on that issue, however. Under the doctrine of stare decisis, this court's prior decisions should not be overturned absent "good cause" or "compelling reasons." *Lindner* engaged in a detailed analysis of the statute's purpose that has been accepted for

Driving*

more than 21 years. *Lindner* should not be overruled without the benefit of a developed argument by the parties on the issue.

We need not overrule *Lindner* to conclude that the license suspensions in this case do not offend due process. We need only apply the highly deferential rational basis standard to decide that the license suspensions do not violate defendants' constitutional rights to due process. The rational basis test is satisfied if there is a conceivable basis for finding a statute rationally related to a legitimate state interest. . . .

In sum, we conclude that suspending defendants' driving privileges for underage consumption of alcohol is rationally related to the legitimate public interest in the safe and legal operation of motor vehicles. Section 6-206(a)(43), as applied in this case, provides a reasonable method of furthering that interest. Accordingly, section 6-206(a)(43) does not violate defendants' constitutional rights to substantive due process.

The Application of the Law Is Not Arbitrary

Defendants also argue section 6-206(a)(43) is unconstitutionally arbitrary as applied because the Secretary does not exercise the discretion granted by the statute in determining whether to suspend a person's driving privileges for underage consumption of alcohol. Rather, the Secretary issues a suspension in every case. Defendants contend the Secretary's failure to exercise discretion is arbitrary and results in a due process violation.

In his reply to this argument, the Secretary contends he does not have discretion in determining whether to suspend a person's driving privileges under section 6-206(a)(43). The Secretary maintains section 6-206(a)(43) requires a three-month suspension when a person receives court supervision for underage consumption of alcohol. . . .

Section 6-206 of the Vehicle Code is entitled, "Discretionary authority to suspend or revoke license or permit; Right to a hearing." Section 6-206 generally authorizes the Secretary to issue a suspension or revocation of driving privileges in 45 enumerated circumstances. In many of those circumstances, the statutory language is purely discretionary. For instance, subsection (a)(3) allows the Secretary to suspend or revoke driving privileges upon a showing that a person has been repeatedly involved in collisions or has repeated traffic offenses indicating an inability to operate a motor vehicle safely or disrespect for traffic laws.

Some states have passed laws that ban teens from driving if they have been charged with underage drinking, even if they were not driving at the time of the incident. © Cultura/Seb Oliver/Getty Images.

Other subsections require specific action by the Secretary, however. In particular, several subsections call for suspension of driving privileges for a certain length of time. . . .

The provision involved in this case, section 6-206(a)(43), states:

> The Secretary of State is authorized to suspend or revoke the driving privileges of any person without preliminary hearing upon a showing of the person's records or other sufficient evidence that the person:
>
> [h]as received a disposition of court supervision for a violation of subsection (a), (d), or (e) of Section 6-20 of the Liquor Control Act of 1934 or a similar provision of a local ordinance, in which case the suspension shall be for a period of 3 months[.]

Similar to the other subsections described above, subsection (a)(43) requires specific action when a person receives court supervision for the underage consumption of alcohol offenses involved here. The statute provides "in which case the suspension shall be for a period of 3 months." Subsection (a)(43) provides for suspension as the only possible action as shown by the phrase "the suspension shall be." The legislature used "the suspension" rather than a less specific reference such as "any suspension." Moreover, the use of "shall be" indicates suspension is the mandatory action. The mandatory nature of the suspension is also shown by the provision of a specific period of three months. The statutory language, therefore, provides for a mandatory consequence of a three-month suspension in these circumstances.

Thus, we conclude the Secretary does not have discretion in determining whether to issue a suspension of defendants' driving privileges under section 6-206(a)(43). Rather, section 6-206(a)(43) provides for mandatory suspension. . . . We must reject defendants' claim that the statute is arbitrary as applied and, therefore, results in a due process violation.

Suspension of Driving Privileges Is Not a Punishment

Finally, defendants renew their argument that suspension of their driving privileges under section 6-206(a)(43) violates the proportionate penalties clause of the Illinois Constitution. Defendants argue that suspension of their driver's licenses, in addition to the criminal penalties imposed for underage consumption of alcohol, results in cruel and degrading punishment.

The proportionate penalties clause in the Illinois Constitution is coextensive with the federal constitution's prohibition of cruel and unusual punishment. Both provisions apply only to the criminal process involving a direct action by the government to inflict punishment. The critical determination, therefore, is whether suspension of the defendants' driving privileges is a direct action by the government to inflict punishment.

We have determined that section 6-206(a)(43)'s purpose is to promote the safe and legal operation and ownership of motor vehicles. Section 6-206(a)(43) is, therefore, intended to provide for safe highways, not to punish licensees for underage consumption of alcohol. Indeed, we have previously stated statutory summary suspension of a driver's license is not penal in nature because it is intended to protect the public rather than punish a licensee. Accordingly, we conclude the proportionate penalties clause does not apply here because suspension of defendants' driving privileges under section 6-206(a)(43) is not a direct action by the government to inflict punishment.

In sum, we conclude that suspension of defendants' driving privileges under section 6-206(a)(43) does not violate their constitutional rights to due process or the proportionate penalties clause. The trial court's orders declaring section 6-206(a)(43) unconstitutional must, therefore, be reversed.

Organizations to Contact

The editors have compiled the following list of organizations con-cerned with the issues debated in this book. The descriptions are derived from materials provided by the organizations. All have publications or information available for interested readers. The list was compiled on the date of publication of the present volume; the information provided here may change. Be aware that many organizations take several weeks or longer to respond to inquiries, so allow as much time as possible.

AAA Digest of Motor Laws

e-mail: digestofmotorlaws@national.aaa.com
website: www.drivinglaws.aaa.com

The AAA Digest of Motor Laws is an online compendium of the motor laws of all US states and Canadian provinces, maintained by the American Automobile Association. It is searchable by topic and by state. Information about different states' laws can also be compared with each other.

AAA Foundation for Traffic Safety

607 Fourteenth Street, NW, Suite 201
Washington, DC 20005
(202) 638-5944 • fax: (202) 638-5943
e-mail: info@aaafoundation.org
website: www.aaafoundation.org

The AAA Foundation for Traffic Safety is a nonprofit organiza-tion founded by the American Automobile Association to iden-tify traffic safety problems, foster research that seeks solutions, and disseminate information and educational materials. Its re-search focuses on safety culture, teen driver safety, senior safety and mobility, and road safety. Its website includes downloadable brochures and many detailed reports on various aspects of these topics, plus video and audio files.

Advocates for Highway and Auto Safety

750 First Street, NE, Suite 901
Washington, DC 20002
(202) 408-1711 • fax: (202) 408-1699
website: www.saferoads.org

Advocates for Highway and Auto Safety is an alliance of consumer, medical, public health, and safety groups and insurance companies and their agents working together to make America's roads safer. It encourages the adoption of federal and state laws, policies, and programs that save lives and reduce injuries. Its website contains news and fact sheets about safety issues and a downloadable road map of state highway safety laws.

Governors Highway Safety Association (GHSA)

444 N. Capitol Street, NW, Suite 722
Washington, DC 20001
(202) 789-0942
e-mail: headquarters@ghsa.org
website: www.ghsa.org

The GHSA is a nonprofit organization representing the state and territorial highway safety offices that implement programs to address behavioral highway safety issues. It provides leadership and advocacy for the states and territories to improve traffic safety, influence national policy, enhance program management, and promote best practices. Its website contains many publications, including some on teen driver safety.

Impact Teen Drivers

PO Box 161209
Sacramento, CA 95816
(916) 733-7432 • fax: (916) 457-3398

e-mail: info@impactteendrivers.org
website: www.impactteendrivers.org

Impact Teen Drivers is a nonprofit organization sponsored by the California Association of Highway Patrolmen, California Casualty, and the California Teachers Association. Its mission is to change the culture of driving forever, thereby saving lives not only in this generation of drivers but also in all future generations through a nationwide educational program that confronts the dangers and consequences of reckless and distracted driving. Its website contains fact sheets, teaching materials, and links, plus many videos, including personal-story videos.

Insurance Institute for Highway Safety (IIHS)
1005 N. Glebe Road, Suite 800
Arlington, VA 22201
(703) 247-1500 • fax: (703) 247-1588
website: www.iihs.org

The IIHS is an independent, nonprofit scientific and educational organization dedicated to reducing the losses—whether deaths, injuries, or property damage—from crashes on the nation's roads. Its Highway Loss Data Institute shares and supports this mission of the thorough scientific study of insurance data representing the human and economic losses resulting from the ownership and operation of different types of vehicles and by publishing insurance loss results by vehicle make and model. The combined website for these two organizations contains a great deal of material related to safe driving, including the details of the graduated driver licensing laws of all the states.

Mothers Against Drunk Driving (MADD)
511 E. John Carpenter Fwy., Suite 700
Irving, TX 75062
(877) 275-6233 • fax: (972) 869-2206
website: www.madd.org

MADD is the nation's largest nonprofit organization working to protect families from drunk driving and underage drinking. It also supports drunk and drugged driving victims and survivors. It supports high-visibility law enforcement to catch drunk drivers and discourage others from driving drunk, and ignition interlock devices for all drunk drivers to prove they are sober before their cars will start. Its website contains information about its goals, tributes to victims, and past issues of its magazine *Maddvocate.*

National Highway Traffic Safety Administration (NHTSA)

1200 New Jersey Ave., SE, West Bldg.
Washington, DC 20590
(888) 327-4236
website: www.nhtsa.gov

The NHTSA is an agency of the US Department of Transportation, established by the Highway Safety Act of 1970 to carry out safety programs under the National Traffic and Motor Vehicle Safety Act of 1966 and the Highway Safety Act of 1966. It sets and enforces safety performance standards for motor vehicles and motor vehicle equipment, and also conducts research on driver behavior and traffic safety. Its website contains detailed statistics and other material about driving safety and about its research projects.

National Safety Council

1121 Spring Lake Drive
Itasca, IL 60143
(800) 621-7615 • fax: (630) 285-1315
website: www.nsc.org

The National Safety Council is a nonprofit organization whose mission is to save lives by preventing injuries and deaths at work, in homes and communities, and on the road through leadership, research, education, and advocacy. It partners with businesses, government agencies, elected officials, and the public to make an impact where the most preventable injuries and deaths occur, in areas such as distracted driving, teen driving, and workplace safety. Most of the material on its website is available only to members; however, there is public access to its magazine *Safety and Health* and a blog for parents of teen drivers at www.teen safedriving.org/blog.

National Youth Rights Association (NYRA)

1101 Fifteenth Street, NW, Suite 200
Washington, DC 20005
(202) 835-1739
website: www.youthrights.org

The National Youth Rights Association is a youth-led national nonprofit organization dedicated to fighting for the civil rights and liberties of young people. NYRA has more than seven thousand members representing all fifty states. It seeks to lower the voting age, lower the drinking age, repeal curfew laws, and protect student rights.

Roadway Safety Foundation

1101 Fourteenth Street, NW, Suite 750
Washington, DC 20005
(202) 857-1228 • fax: (202) 857-1220
e-mail: info@roadwaysafety.org
website: www.roadwaysafety.org

The Roadway Safety Foundation is a nonprofit educational and charitable organization chartered in 1995 by the American Highway Users Alliance. Its mission is to reduce the frequency and severity of motor vehicle crashes, injuries, and fatalities by improving the physical characteristics of America's roadways— design and engineering, operating conditions, removal of road-side hazards, and the effective use of safety features. Its website contains information about its programs and accomplishments, plus descriptions of materials from its educational campaigns, of which free copies can be ordered by e-mail.

Safe Teen Driving Club

10 Glenlake Pkwy. NE
Atlanta, GA 30328
(678) 820-8630
e-mail: info@safeteendrivingclub.org
website: www.safeteendrivingclub.org

The Safe Teen Driving Club works with parents to help educate, mentor, manage, and monitor their teen drivers. It provides parents of teen drivers with tools, services, and technology solutions for monitoring the driving habits of their young drivers. Its website contains an educational blog on topics such as teen car insurance and teen GPS tracking.

University of North Carolina Highway Safety Research Center

730 Martin Luther King Jr. Blvd.
CB# 3430
Chapel Hill, NC 27599
(919) 962-2202 • fax: (919) 962-8710
website: www.hsrc.unc.edu

The University of North Carolina Highway Safety Research Center is a leading research institute that has helped shape the field of transportation safety. Its mission is to improve the safety, security, access, and efficiency of all surface transportation modes through a balanced, interdisciplinary program of research, evaluation, and information dissemination. Its website contains bibliographies of research reports with links to those available online.

For Further Reading

Books

Alliance for Safe Driving, *License to Drive*. Independence, KY: Cengage, 2007.

Phil Berardelli, *Safe Young Drivers: A Guide for Parents and Teens*. Mountain Lake Park, MD: Mountain Lake Press, 2008.

Robert H. Deatherage, *Survival Driving: Staying Alive on the World's Most Dangerous Roads*. Boulder, CO: Paladin, 2006.

Brett Elkins and Bruce Elkins, *Teach Your Teen to Drive . . . and Stay Alive*. North Charleston, SC: CreateSpace, 2012.

Karen Gravelle, *The Driving Book: Everything New Drivers Need to Know but Don't Know to Ask*. New York: Walker, 2005.

Tim Hollister, *Not So Fast: Parenting Your Teen Through the Dangers of Driving*. Chicago: Chicago Review Press, 2013.

Margaret L. Johnson, Owen Crabb, Arthur A. Opfer, Randall R. Thiel, and Frederik R. Mottola, *Drive Right: You Are the Driver*. Upper Saddle River, NJ: Prentice Hall, 2007.

Michael R. Kahn and Robert B. Lacorte, *Don't Die in a Car: Simple Tips for Staying Out of Automobile Accidents*. North Charleston, SC: CreateSpace, 2013.

Joanne Mallon, *How to Overcome Fear of Driving: The Road to Driving Confidence*. United Kingdom: Nell James, 2012.

Responsible Driving, Student Edition. Woodland Hills, CA: McGraw-Hill/Glencoe, 2006.

Timothy C. Smith, *Crash-Proof Your Kids: Make Your Teen a Safer, Smarter Driver*. New York: Touchstone, 2006.

Periodicals and Internet Resources

Michael Aisenberg, "Driving *Is* a Privilege," Safe Teen Driving Club, July 20, 2012. www.safeteendrivingclub.org.

Abby Barsky, "Incapacitated Teen Drivers Endanger Communities and Lives," *The Chariot*, Johns Creek High School (GA), February 28, 2013. www.jchschariot.com.

Ramona M. Carlos et al., "Survey Explores Teen Driving Behavior in Central Valley, Los Angeles High Schools," *University of California Agriculture*, October–December 2009. www.ucanr.edu.

John Cichowski, "Road Warrior: Report Rekindles Debate over Teen Decal," NorthJersey.com, October 28, 2012. www .northjersey.com.

Jim Ellis, "Punishing Minor Consumption by Suspending Their Driver's License," *Legal Contemplations* (blog), September 12, 2012. www.legalcontemplations.blogspot.com.

Teri Figueroa, "Teens, Driving and a 'Silly, Stupid Decision,'" *San Diego Union-Tribune*, April 21, 2013. www.utsandiego .com.

Marie Hartwell-Walker, "Teens, Texting and Driving: Disaster in the Making," PsychCentral, January 30, 2013. www .psychcentral.com.

Highway Loss Data Institute, "Drop in Teen Driving Tracks with Teen Unemployment, HLDI Study Finds," *HLDI News*, October 24, 2013. www.iihs.org.

Randye Hodery, "Yo, I'm Driving. I'll Text You When It's Safe," *Motherlode* (blog), NYTimes.com, September 25, 2013. http://parenting.blogs.nytimes.com.

Insurance Institute for Highway Safety, "N.J. Teen Decals Boost Citations, Not Compliance," *IIHS Status Report*, December 15, 2011. www.iihs.org.

Insurance Institute for Highway Safety, "States Could Sharply Reduce Teen Crash Deaths by Strengthening Graduated Driver Licensing Laws," *IIHS News*, May 31, 2012. www.iihs .org.

Alex Koroknay-Palicz, "The STANDUP Act Is a Big Mistake," *Huffington Post*, June 4, 2010. www.huffingtonpost .com.

Tanya Kurepina, Sierra Lai, and Walter Payton, "Teens Pump the Brakes on Getting Their Driver's Licenses, *Huffington Post*, January 30, 2014. www.huffingtonpost.com.

Marianne Lavelle, "US Teenagers Are Driving Much Less: 4 Theories About Why," *National Geographic* Daily News, December 17, 2013. http://news.nationalgeographic.com.

Allison Linn, "Teens Waiting Longer to Take the Wheel," NBC News, July 12, 2013. www.nbcnews.com.

Ashley Mackenzie, "What Is the History of the Driver's License?," eHow, no date. www.ehow.com.

Mary Madden and Amanda Lenhart, "Teens and Distracted Driving," Pew Research Center, November 16, 2009. www .pewinternet.org.

Mike Males, "California's Graduated Driver License Law: Effects on Older Teenagers," *Californian Journal of Health Promotion*, September 2006. www.cjhp.org.

Mike Males, "More Dangerous than Anyone Thought," Fairness and Accuracy in Reporting, October 1, 2006. www.fair.org.

Scott V. Masten, Robert D. Foss, and Stephen W. Marshall, "Graduated Driver Licensing and Fatal Crashes Involving 16- to 19-Year-Old Drivers," *JAMA: The Journal of the American Medical Association*, September 14, 2011. http:// jama.jamanetwork.com.

National Safety Council, "Understanding the Distracted Brain," March 2010. www.nsc.org.

Anahad O'Connor, "Teenage Driving Laws May Just Delay Deadly Crashes," *Well* (blog), NYTimes.com, September 14, 2011. http://well.blogs.nytimes.com.

Orlando Sentinel, "Blood in the Streets," July 2013. www.orlando sentinel.com/news/local/pedestrian-deaths-central-florida.

Karen Osborne, "A Lesson for Teens or Anyone: Texting While Driving Kills," CatholicPhilly.com, December 28, 2012. www.catholicphilly.com.

Kelly Petryszen, "Spare a Life: Mother Uses Son's Death to Warn Others to Stop Texting While Driving," *Morning Journal* (Lorain, OH), September 2, 2012. www.morningjournal .com.

Scott Remer, "Texting While Driving: Why the Controversy?," *The Beachcomber: Online*, Beachwood High School (OH), March 11, 2010. www.bcomber.org.

Brian C. Tefft, Allan F. Williams, and Jurek G. Grabowski, "Teen Driver Risk in Relation to Age and Number of Passengers," AAA Foundation for Traffic Safety, May 2012. www.aaa foundation.org.

Lyxan Toledanes, "After Texting Accident, Teen Wants to Be Advocate for Life," *Odessa (TX) American*, August 27, 2012. www.oaoa.com.

Index